Ordnance Survey Ireland

3rd Edition

DUBLIN
CITY CENTRE
STREET ATLAS

GW00418732

CONTENTS

CITY CENTRE TERMINUS GUIDE
LEGEND

Compiled and published by Ordnance Survey Ireland, Phoenix Park, Dublin 8, Ireland.

Unauthorised reproduction infringes Ordnance Survey Ireland and Government of Ireland copyright. All rights reserved. No part of this publication may be copied, reproduced or transmitted in any form or by any means without the prior written permission of the copyright owners.

© Ordnance Survey Ireland 2005

Arna thiomsú agus arna fhoilsiú ag Suirbhéireacht Ordanáis Éireann, Páirc an Fhionnuisce, Baile Átha Cliath 8, Éire. Sáraíonn atáirgeadh neamhúdaraithe cóipcheart Shuirbhéireacht Ordanáis Éireann agus Rialtas na hÉireann. Gach cead ar cosnamh. Ní ceadmhach aon chuid den fhoilseachán seo a chóipeáil, a atáirgeadh nó a tharchur in aon fhoirm ná ar aon bhealach gan cead i scríbhinn roimh ré ó úinéirí an chóipchirt.

© Suirbhéireacht Ordanáis Éireann 2005

Printed by the Print Consortium of Ireland.
SPECIAL THANKS TO O.P.W. THE HERITAGE SERVICE

Dublin Bus
Serving the entire community

CITY CENTRE TERMINI and MAIN BUS STOPS

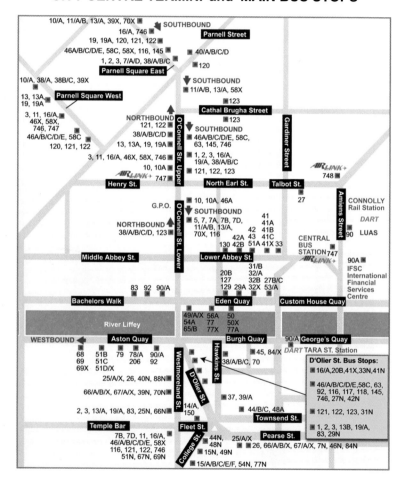

10/A, 11/A/B, 13/A, 39X, 70X
16/A, 746 — SOUTHBOUND
Parnell Street
19, 19A, 120, 121, 122
46A/B/C/D/E, 58C, 58X, 116, 145
40/A/B/C/D
1, 2, 3, 7/A/D, 38/A/B/C
Parnell Square East
120

10/A, 38/A, 38B/C, 39X
SOUTHBOUND
11/A/B, 13/A, 58X
13, 13A,
19, 19A
Parnell Square West
123
Cathal Brugha Street
3, 11, 16/A,
46X, 58X,
746, 747
123
46A/B/C/D/E, 58C
120, 121, 122

NORTHBOUND
121, 122
O'Connell Str. Upper
SOUTHBOUND
38/A/B/C/D
46A/B/C/D/E, 58C,
63, 145, 746
13, 13A, 19, 19A
1, 2, 3, 16/A,
19/A, 38/A/B/C
3, 11, 16/A, 46X, 58X, 746
10, 10A
121, 122, 123
AIRLINK+ 747
Henry St.
North Earl St.
Talbot St.
Gardiner Street
AIRLINK+ 748

G.P.O.
10, 10A, 46A
SOUTHBOUND
5, 7, 7A, 7B, 7D,
11/A/B, 13/A,
70X, 116
41
41A
41B
41C
42 43
42A 51A 41X 33
130 43
NORTHBOUND
38/A/B/C/D, 123
O'Connell Str. Lower
27
Amiens Street
CONNOLLY
Rail Station
DART
LUAS
90
CENTRAL
BUS
STATION 747
AIRLINK+

Middle Abbey St.
Lower Abbey St.
90A
IFSC
International
Financial
Services
Centre

83 92 90/A
31/B
32/A
20B
127 32B 27B/C
129 29A 32X 53/A
Bachelors Walk
Eden Quay
Custom House Quay

River Liffey
49/A/X 56A 50
54A 77 50X
65/B 77X 77A

WESTBOUND ◄
Aston Quay
Burgh Quay
90/A **George's Quay**
DART TARA ST. Station
68 51B 79 78/A 90/A
69 51C 206 92
69X 51D/X
45, 84/X
38/A/B/C, 70
25/A/X, 26, 40N, 88N
66/A/B/X, 67/A/X, 39N, 70N
37, 39/A
2, 3, 13/A, 19/A, 83, 25N, 66N
44/B/C, 48A
Townsend St.
Westmoreland St.
D'Olier St.
Hawkins St.
14/A,
150

D'Olier St. Bus Stops:
16/A,20B,41X,33N,41N
46/A/B/C/D/E,58C, 63,
92, 116, 117, 118, 145,
746, 27N, 42N
121, 122, 123, 31N
1, 2, 3, 13B, 19/A,
83, 29N

Temple Bar
7B, 7D, 11, 16/A,
46/A/B/C/D/E, 58X
116, 121, 122, 746
51N, 67N, 69N
Fleet St.
44N
48N
15N, 49N
25/A/X
Pearse St.
26, 66/A/B/X, 67/A/X, 7N, 46N, 84N
College St.
15/A/B/C/E/F, 54N, 77N

LEGEND

▬▬▬	**MAIN ROADS/ STREETS**	🐾 *WATER*		ℹ️	**TOURIST OFFICE**
✕ 8 / 3	**OTHER ROADS/ STREETS** (UNNAMED)	🎾	**TENNIS**	⛲	**INDEPENDENT HOSTEL**
▬▬▬	**NARROW / STREET PRIVATE ROADS**	🎭	**THEATRE**	▲	**AN ÓIGE HOSTEL**
▬▬▬	**PEDESTRIAN STREETS**	🎬	**CINEMA**	PO	**POST OFFICE**
▬ ▬ ▬	**TUNNEL UNDER CONSTRUCTION**	🛍️	**SHOPPING COMPLEX**	🅿️	**PARKING**
▬▬▬	**RAILWAY**	🎨	**ART GALLERY**	★	**GARDA**
▬ ▬ ▬	**LUAS LINE**	Ω	**MUSEUM**	🔥	**FIRE STATION**
─ ─ ─	**WAYMARKED WALK**	◀	**VISITOR CENTRE**	DART ARROW	**SUBURBAN RAIL STATIONS**
▭	**BUILT UP AREA**	📖	**LIBRARY**	○	**LUAS STATION**
▭	**GREEN SPACE**	✝	**CHURCH OF NOTE**	⚡	**MAINLINE RAIL STATION**
▭	**PUBLIC PARK**	🏢	**BUILDING OF SPECIAL INTEREST**	E	**EMERGENCY HOSPITAL**
	PUBLIC BUILDING	🎓	**3RD LEVEL INST.**	◀▬	**ONE WAY TRAFFIC SYSTEM**
▲	**RAIL/ BUS STATION**	⚫	**GAELIC GROUND**	†	**CHURCH**
	BUILDING OF NOTE	🏉	**RUGBY GROUND**	⊓	**PRAYER HALL**
	HOSPITAL	⚽	**SOCCER GROUND**	⛴️	**CAR FERRY**
				✈	**AIRPORT**

SCALE 1:10 000
(1 cm = 100 metres) 100m 50m 0 metres 100m 200m 300m 400m 500 metres

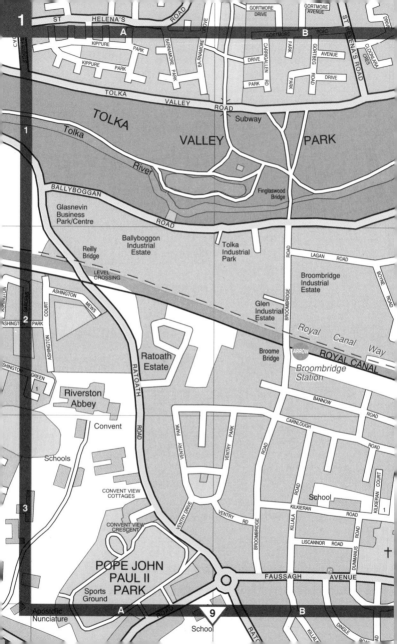

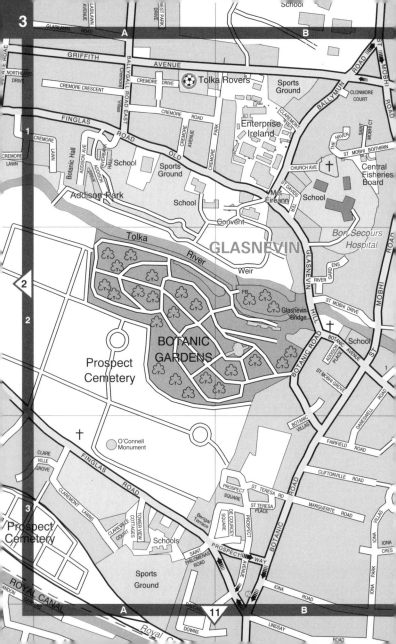

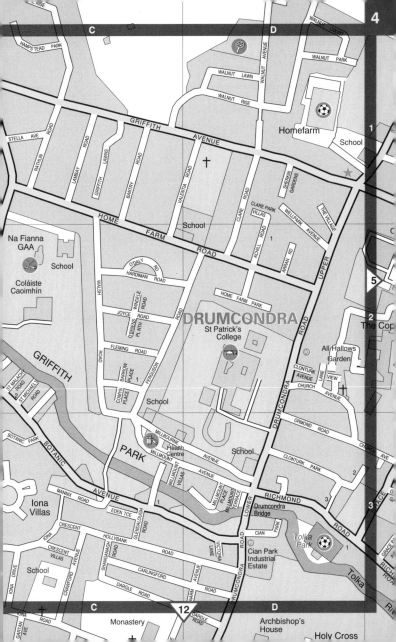

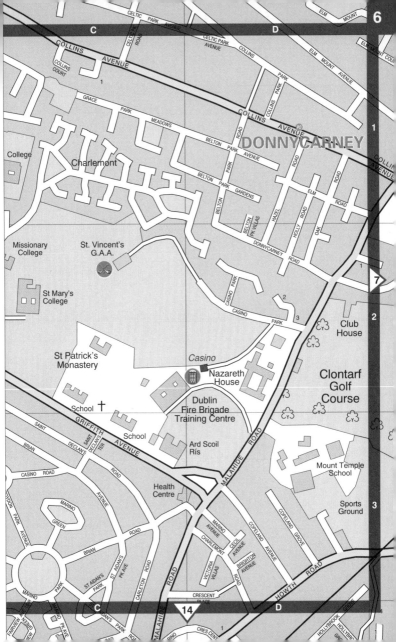

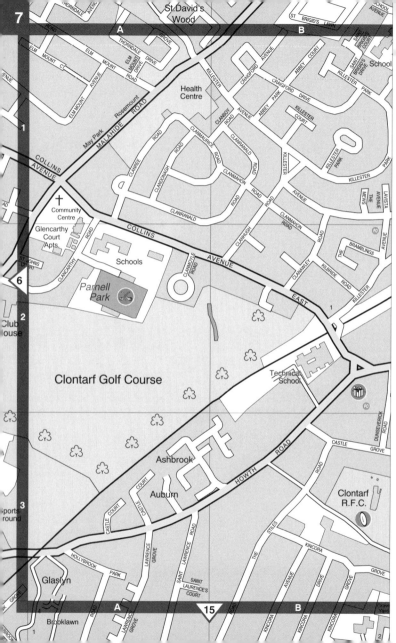

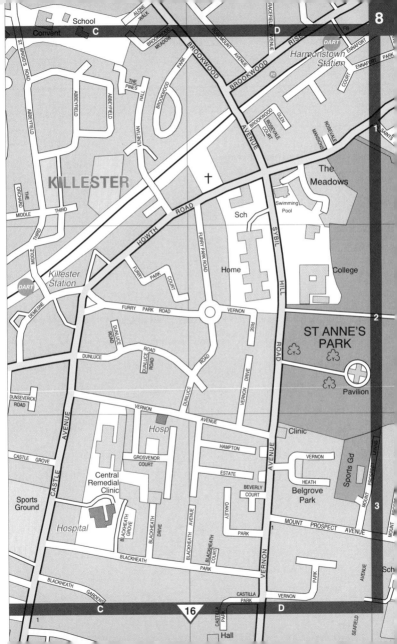

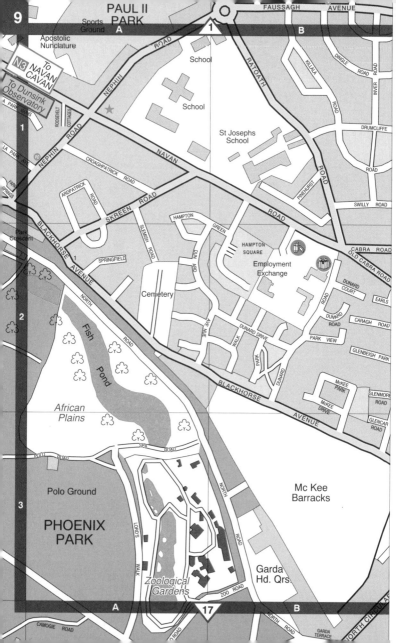

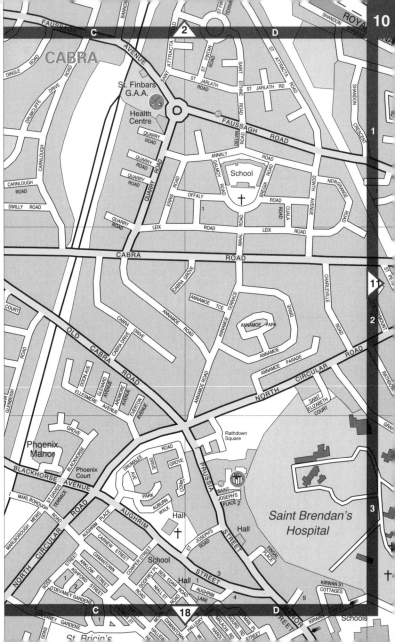

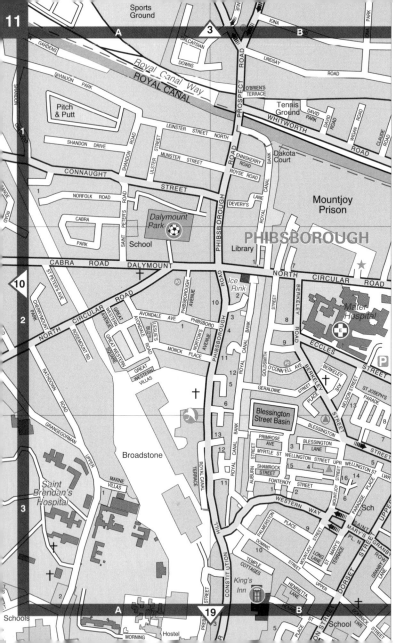

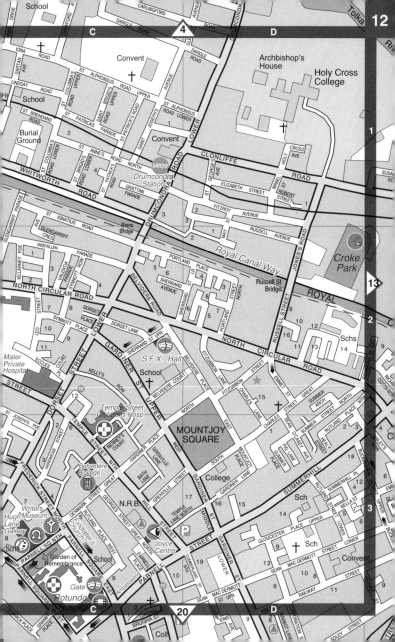

ST AIDAN'S
PARK
ST AIDA
PK AVE
VICTOR
VILLAS
AVE
CRESCENT
PLACE
CHARLEMONT ROAD

PARK AVE
DOLLETON ROAD
HOWTH ROAD
MALAHIDE ROAD

FAIRVIEW AVE UPR
GREEN
MARINO
ST AIDAN'S PARK ROAD

HOLLYBROOK GROVE
HOLLYBROOK
GROVE

FAIR
School
HAVERTY ROAD
College
MARINO
CRESCENT

STRANDVILLE AVENUE EAST

BROOK
LAWN

MERVILLE
AVENUE
Marino Mart
Marino
College
FAIRVIEW
School
✝

1

FAIRVIEW
FB
Clontarf
Road Station
CLONTARF
ROAD

**FAIRVIEW
PARK**
DART
Traffic
School

Running
Track

15

2

ROAD

BYRNE

ALFIE
John McCormack
Bridge
BOUNDARY ROAD

PORTSIDE
COURT
EAST
Portside
Business
Centre
East Point
Business Park

SEAVIEW AVENUE EAST
SEAVIEW
AVE

WALL

EAST WALL

CHURCH ROAD
BARDY ROAD
FORTH ROAD

3

ROAD

SHELMALIER ROAD
RAVENSDALE ROAD
PORT
TUNNELL

CALEDON
ROAD
CALEDON ROAD

BOND ROAD

SAINT MARY'S ROAD

1
School
Docklands
Innovation
Park

EAST ROAD
MERCHANT'S ROAD

Harbour
Police

Community
Centre
IDA Small
Industry Centre
East Road
Industrial Estate
TOLKA QUAY

KILLA
ROAD
CHURCH

LC

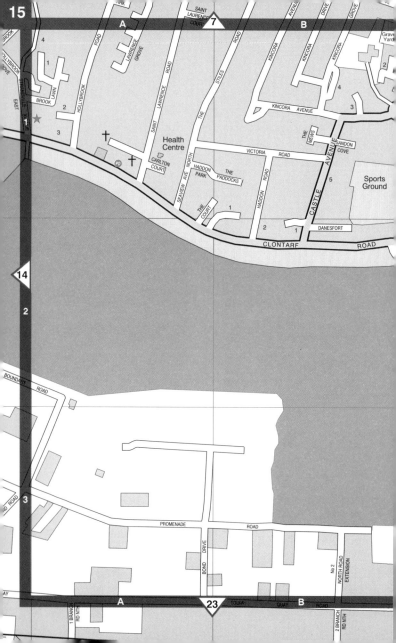

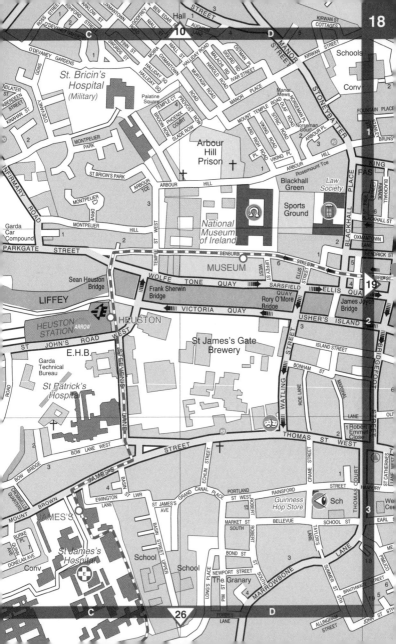

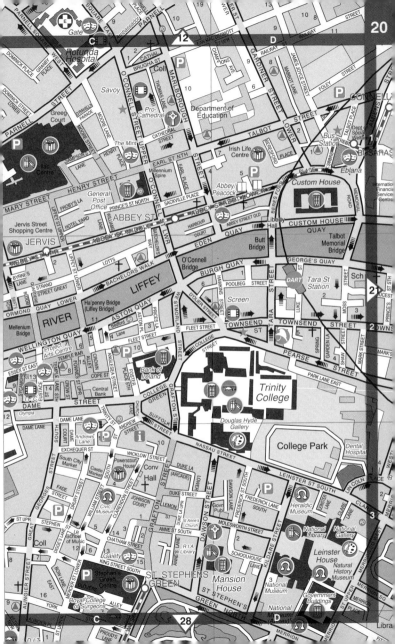

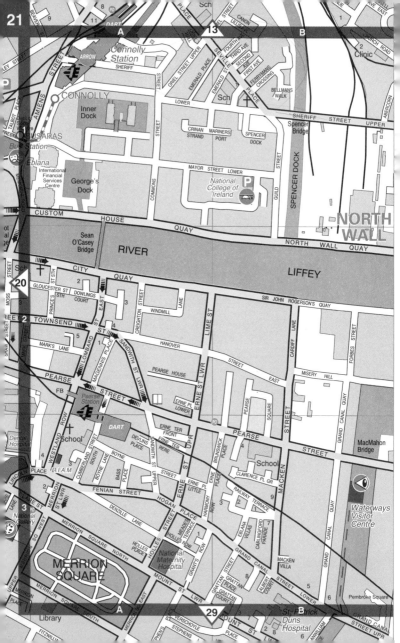

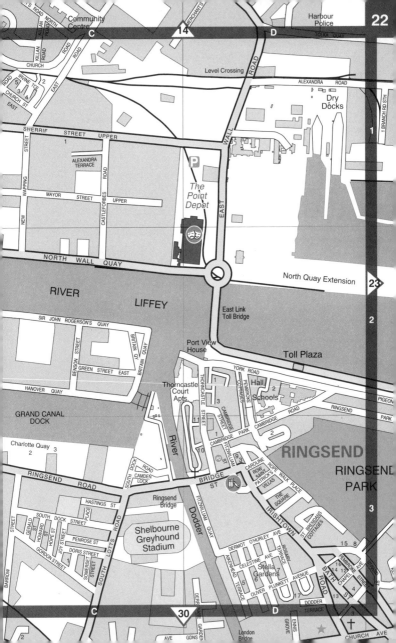

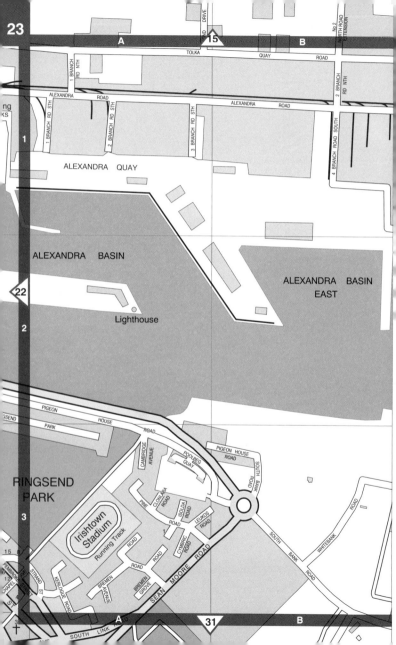

A 15 B

No 2
NORTH ROAD
EXTENSION

TOLKA   QUAY   ROAD

1 BRANCH RD NTH

2 BRANCH RD NTH

ALEXANDRA   ROAD

ALEXANDRA   ROAD

1

1 BRANCH RD STH

2 BRANCH RD STH

3 BRANCH RD STH

4 BRANCH ROAD SOUTH

ng
KS

ALEXANDRA   QUAY

ALEXANDRA   BASIN

22

2

Lighthouse

ALEXANDRA   BASIN
EAST

PIGEON   HOUSE   ROAD

GSEND

PIGEON HOUSE
ROAD

PARK

CAMBRIDGE AVENUE

POOLBEG
QUAY

SOUTH BANK ROAD

RINGSEND
PARK

PINE ROAD

CLONLIFFE ROAD

ISOLDA ROAD

LEUKOS ROAD

ROAD

WHITEBANK ROAD

3

Irishtown
Stadium

Running Track

ROAD

CYMRIC ROAD

SEAN MOORE ROAD

SOUTH BANK ROAD

ROAD

15 8

PERIWINKLE

STRAND ST

KERLOGUE ROAD

BREMEN AVENUE

BREMEN GROVE

CHAPEL

3

SOUTH   LINK   RING

A 31 B

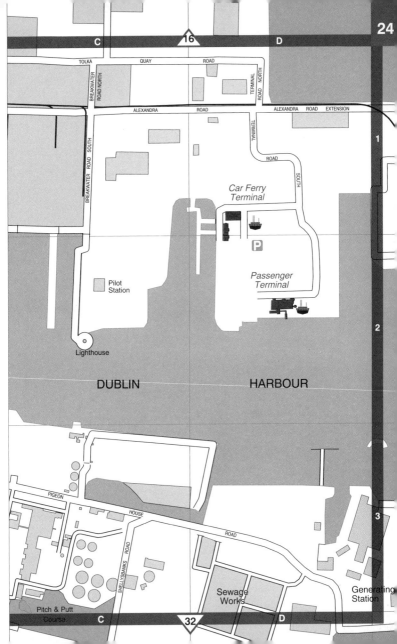

C
16
D

TOLKA QUAY ROAD

BREAKWATER ROAD NORTH

TERMINAL ROAD NORTH

ALEXANDRA ROAD

ALEXANDRA ROAD EXTENSION

1

BREAKWATER ROAD SOUTH

TERMINAL

ROAD

SOUTH

Car Ferry Terminal

P

Pilot Station

Passenger Terminal

2

Lighthouse

DUBLIN

HARBOUR

PIGEON

HOUSE

3

SHELLYBANKS ROAD

ROAD

Sewage Works

Generating Station

Pitch & Putt Course

C
32
D

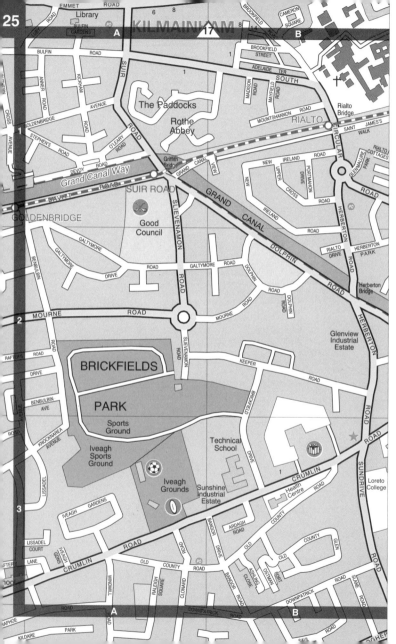

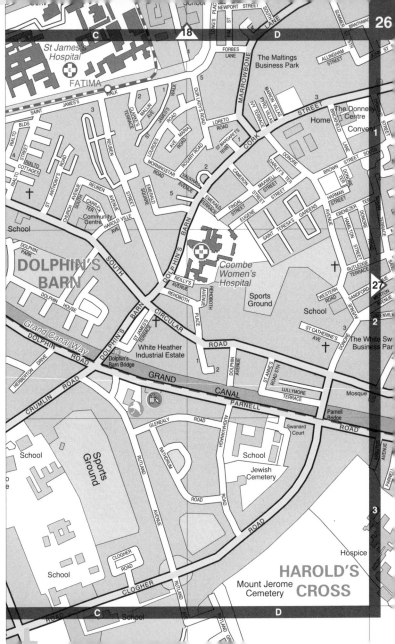

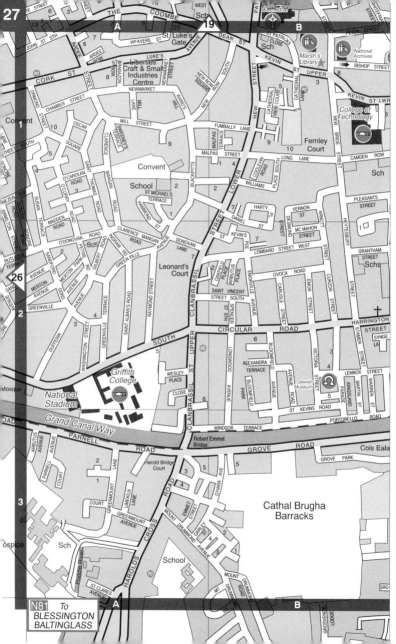

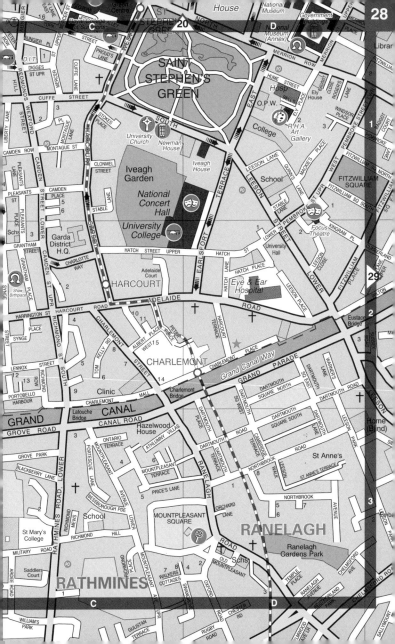

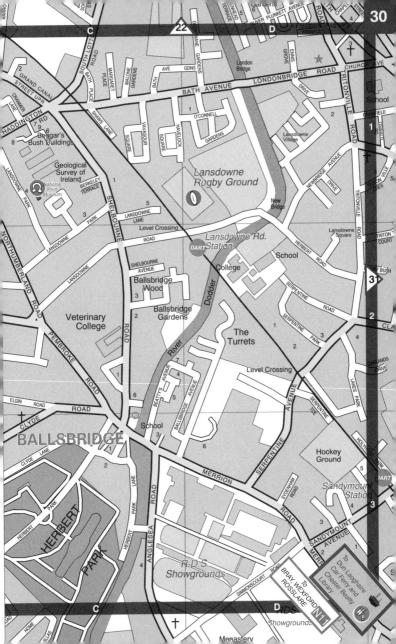

C 22 **D**

School

CHAPEL STREET

CITY QUAY TERRACE

London Bridge

LONDONBRIDGE ROAD

CHURCH AVE

TRITONVILLE ROAD

CRASSFIELD

GRAND CANAL STREET UPR

HADDINGTON RD

Beggar's Bush Buildings

Geological Survey of Ireland

National Print Museum

SOUTH LOTTS ROAD

BATH PLACE

MARGARET PLACE

MALONE GARDENS

BATH AVE GDNS

O'CONNELL GARDENS

SHAWS LANE

SQUARE

VAVASOUR SQUARE

HAVELOCK SQUARE

GARDENS

Lansdowne Village

BATH AVENUE

ENNIS GROVE

Lansdowne Rugby Ground

New Bridge

NEWBRIDGE AVENUE

Lansdowne Square

TRITONVILLE ROAD

TRITON COURT

TRITONVILLE MEWS

BERKELEY TERRACE

SHELBOURNE LANE

LANSDOWNE

PARK

LANSDOWNE

NORTHUMBERLAND ROAD

SHELBOURNE ROAD

Level Crossing

LANSDOWNE ROAD

Lansdowne Rd. Station **DART**

College

School

HERBERT ROAD

SHELBOURNE AVENUE

Ballsbridge Wood

Ballsbridge Gardens

Veterinary College

SERPENTINE AVENUE

SERPENTINE ROAD

SERPENTINE PARK

BERRY BUSH

CLA

PEMBROKE ROAD

ROAD

River Dodder

The Turrets

Level Crossing

OAKLANDS DRIVE

LANGS PARK

ELGIN ROAD

ROAD

CLYDE ROAD

BEATTY'S AVENUE

BALLSBRIDGE AVENUE

School

SERPENTINE AVENUE

SERPENTINE TCE

HOLLYBROOK PARK

DART

CLYDE LANE

BALLSBRIDGE

LANE

MERRION ROAD

Hockey Ground

Sandymount Station

HERBERT

PARK

HERBERT PARK

PARK

ANGLESEA ROAD

SYDENHAM ROAD

SANDYMOUNT AVENUE

HERBERT

CLYDE

HOME VILLAS

R.D.S. Showgrounds

SIMMONSCOURT ROAD

BRAY WEXFORD ROSSLARE

To Dun Laoghaire Car Ferry and Chester Beatty Library

N11

Monastery

Showgrounds

C **D**

31

2

3

1

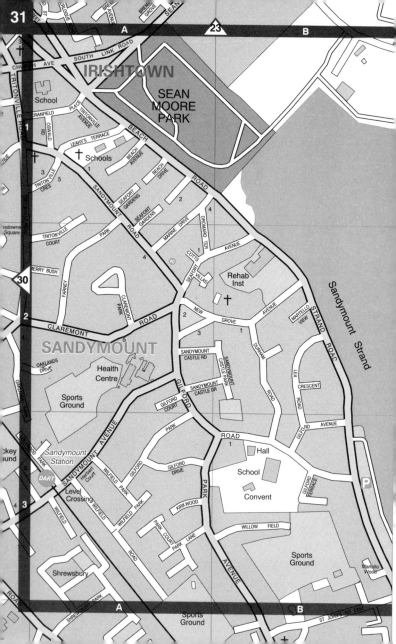

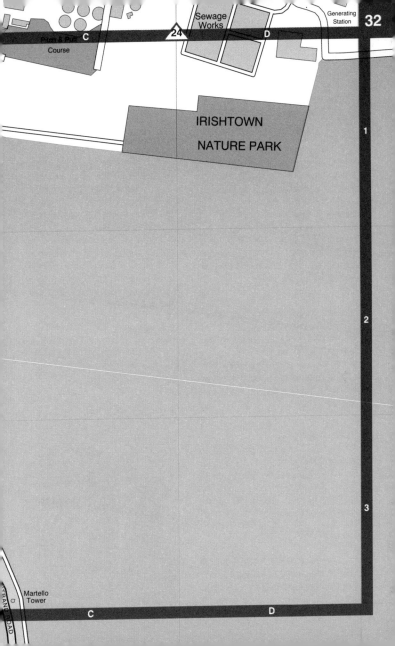

Sewage
Works

Generating
Station

Pitch & Putt
Course

C

24

D

IRISHTOWN

NATURE PARK

1

2

3

Martello
Tower

C

D

TOURIST INFORMATION
Buildings of Note

Bank of Ireland (Former Parliament House)
College Green
Designed by Sir Edward Lovett Pearce and built between 1729 and 1739. Enlarged by James Gandon and Robert Parke between 1785 and 1794. The Bank of Ireland took over this building in 1804. It had been the scene of many dramatic events in Irish politics up to the passing of the Act of Union in 1800
Visiting Times:
Mon, Tues, Wed, Fri 10a.m. - 4p.m.
Thurs 10a.m. - 5p.m.
House of Lords Tours (except bank Hol's)
Tues. 10.30a.m., 11.30a.m. and 1.45p.m.
Bank of Ireland Arts Centre
Tues - Fri 10a.m. - 4p.m.   **20 C2**

Belvedere House/Belvedere College
Great Denmark Street
Built in 1775 for George Rochford Lord Belvedere. It was bought in 1841 by the Jesuits for use as a boys college. The building contains some fine plasterwork by Michael Stapleton and fireplaces by the Venetian Bossi.   **12 C3**

Bluecoat School
Blackhall Place
Designed by Thomas Ivory and built in the palladian style between 1773 and 1783. The Interior has some fine plasterwork by Charles Thorp. The cupola was added in 1904. It is now the home of the Incorporated Law Society.   **18 D1**

Brazen Head
Lower Bridge Street
This is Dublin's oldest hostelery built in 1666. Its foundations which are at a lower level than the surrounding area suggest that it was built on a much older site probably Viking. Its was frequented by many Irish patriots including Wolfe Tone, Robert Emmet and Daniel O'Connell.   **19 A2**

Casino Marino
Malahide Road
Located 4kms from the city centre off the Malahide Road. The Casino was built in 1758 for Lord Charlemont from a design by Sir William Chambers. It has been described as one of the finest 18th century classical buildings in Ireland. Access is by guided tour only
Visiting Times:
November - March
12 noon - 4p.m. Sat. / Sun.
April 12 noon - 5p.m. Sat. / Sun.
May and October
10a.m. - 5p.m. Daily
June - September
10a.m. - 6p.m. Daily   **6 D2**

Casino Marino

City Hall
Cork Hill

Formerly the Royal Exchange, designed by Thomas Cooley and completed between 1769 and 1779.

This is the headquarters for Dublin's Municipal Government. Archives dating back to the 12th Century are stored in the Muniment Room. It also houses the mace and sword of the city along with 102 Royal Charters.

Visiting Times:
Mon - Sat 10a.m. - 5.15p.m.
Sun and Bank Holiday's 2p.m. - 5p.m.
19 **B2**

The Royal College of Surgeons,
St Stephen's Green West.

Designed by William Murray and built between 1825 and 1827. It was occupied by the Irish Citizen Army during the 1916 Rising under the command of Countess Markievicz. 20 **C3**

The Customs House
Custom House Quay

Designed by James Gandon and built between 1781 and 1791. The building was gutted by fire during the War of Independence. It was restored by the Office of Public Works after the Irish Free State was established. 20 **D1**

Dublin Castle

Built at the behest of King John in 1204 on a site which was once a Viking stronghold. It has served as a military fortress, prison, courts of law and the core of British Administration in Ireland until 1922. The Castle is now used for State functions. Guided tours of the State Apartments, Chapel Royal and Undercroft.

Visiting Times:
Mon - Fri 10a.m. - 4.45p.m.
Sat/Sun/Public Holidays 2p.m. 4.45p.m.

Closed 24th - 26th December, 1st January and Good Friday. Last admission 15mins before closing. NOTE Sate appartments are occassionally closed for State Functions. 19 **B3**

General Post Office
O'Connell Street

Designed by Francis Johnston and built between 1814 and 1818.

The GPO became the focal point of the 1916 Insurrection and the Proclamation of the Irish Republic took place there.

Destroyed by fire, it was restored in 1929. In the publc office is a noteworthy statue representing the Death of Cuchulainn, the work of Oliver Sheppard R.H.A. 20 **C1**

The Four Courts
Inns Quay

Built between 1785 and 1802 this is one of designer James Gandon's masterpieces. It houses the Irish Law Courts and Law Library. Destroyed by fire in 1922 it was completely restored in 1932. 19 **B2**

Dublin Castle

Government Buildings,
Upper Merrion Street

This building was designed as the Royal College of Science by Sir Aston Webb. It was opened by King George V on his visit in 1911. The Taoiseach's and some other ministerial offices are located here.
Visiting times:
Saturday 10.30a.m. - 3p.m. departing every 30mins. Tours start at the National Gallery. Last tour starts at 2.15p.m. 20 **D3**

Iveagh House,
St Stephen's Green.

This building built in 1736 was presented to the Irish Nation in 1939 by the 2nd Earl Iveagh. It is now occupied by the Department of Foreign Affairs.   28 **D1**

Kilmainham Gaol
Inchicore Road

One of the largest decommissioned jails in Europe, it played its part in some of the most partriotic and tragic episodes that light the path of Ireland's journey to modern nationhood, from the 1780s to 1924. Featuring many exhibitions and a multi-lingual audio-visual show. Access by guided tour only.
Visiting Times:
Oct - March
Mon - Sat 9.30a.m. - 5.30p.m.
Sun 10a.m. - 6p.m.
April - Sept
9.30a.m. - 6p.m. Daily
Last admission 1.15 before closing.
Closed 24th - 26th December   17 **A3**

Kings Inn
Constitution Hill

Designed partly by James Gandon and built between 1795 and 1817. The Library contains 100,000 volumes including most of the Dublin directories published and a fine collection of English county histories. Not open to the public.   11 **B3**

Leinster House
Kildare Street

Designed by Richard Cassells this fine Georgian town house was built for the Duke of Leinster. The Royal Dublin Society occupied it until 1922 when it was purchased by the Irish Free State. Since 1922 it has served as a Parliament House which is the meeting place of the Dail (Chamber of Deputies) and Seanad (Senate).   20 **D3**

The Mansion House
Dawson Street

This Queen Anne style house designed by Joshua Dawson was built in 1710. The round room was added in 1821. It has been the official residence of Dublin's Lord Mayors since 1715. The Anglo-Irish truce was signed here in 1921.   20 **D3**

Newman House
85 - 86 St Stephen's Green.

The Catholic University (now U.C.D.) founded here by Cardinal Newman. The poet Gerard Manley Hopkins was professor of Greek here while James Joyce and Flann O'Brien studied here.
These two fine 18th century houses have been restored and are open to the public.

28 **C1**

Georgian Door

"Number 29"
Georgian House Museum
Lower Fitzwilliam Street
Situated on the corner of Mount Street
and Fitzwilliam Street. This typical middle-
class home of the period 1790 - 1820 is
faithfully restored and furnished.
Visiting Times:
Tues - Sat 10a.m. - 5p.m.
Sunday 1p.m. - 5p.m.
Closed Mondays, Good Friday and
two weeks before Christmas.   29 **A1**

Powerscourt House
South William Street
Designed by Robert Mack for Viscount
Powerscourt and built between 1771 and
1774. It is now a shopping mall including
cafes, restaurants, crafts and antiques.
                                    20 **C3**

The Rotunda Hospital
Parnell Square
The Rotunda Hospital was the first
purpose built maternity hospital in the
British Isles. Designed by Richard
Bassels it was opened in 1757. A feature
of the building is its chapel with its fine
baroque plasterwork by Bartholomew
Cranmillion.   20 **C1**

Royal Hospital and Irish Museum of
Modern Art
Military Road, Kilmainham
This the most important 17th century
building in Ireland has recently been
restored. Guided tours available of the
Master's Quarters, the Great Hall with the
portrait collection, and the chapel which
contains outstanding woodcarving by
Tabary and a magnificent Baroque ceil-
ing. The Irish Museum of Modern Art was
established in 1991 and exhibits Irish and
International art of the 20th century

Visiting Times:
Tues - Sat 10a.m. - 5.30p.m.
Wed 10.30a.m. - 5.30p.m.
Sun/Public Holiday 12noon - 5.30p.m.
Closed Monday's, Good Friday, 24th -
26th December,
Last admission 5.15p.m.   17 **B3**

The Shaw Birthplace
Synge Street
Situated at No. 33 Synge Street this is the
birthplace of George Bernard Shaw the
Nobel prizewinning author and play-
wright. Built in 1838 it also gives an
insight into the life of a Victorian family.
Visiting Times:
May - Sept
Mon - Sat 10a.m. - 5p.m.
Sundays and PublicHolidays 11a.m. - 5p.m.
Closed for lunch 1pm - 2p.m.   28 **C2**

Tailors' Hall
High Street
Built in 1706 - 1707 this is Dublin's only
surviving guildhall. Restored in recent
times, it now houses An Taisce the Irish
National Trust.
Visiting Times:
By appointment only. Phone 4541786
                                    19 **B3**

Trinity College
College Green
Trinity is a one college university founded
by Queen Elizabeth in 1592. The oldest
buildings now surviving date from 1700.
The multi-media presentation "The Dublin
Experience" in on show from May to
September.
Visiting Times:
Mon - Sat 10a.m. - 5p.m.
See also Trinity College Library   20 **D2**

Parks and Gardens

Garden of Remembrance
Parnell Square East, Dublin 1
The Garden of Remembrance was designed by Daithí Hanly and is dedicated to the memory of those who died in the cause of Irish freedom. The garden is open daily during daylight hours.   12 **C3**

Herbert Park
Ballsbridge
A charming mature park, well laid out with interesting trees, shrubs and flower beds. An attractive feature is the large pond on the eastern side of the park.   30 **C3**

Irish National War Memorial Park
Islandbridge
Designed by the English architect Sir Edward Lutyens, these gardens are dedicated to the memory of 49,400 Irish soldiers who died in the First World War. The Gardens are open every day all year round during daylight hours.   17 **A2**

Merrion Square Park
Merrion Square
Formerly only for the use of the residents of Merrion Square, this public park is surrounded on all sides by some of Dublin's finest Georgian architecture.
21 **A3**

National Botanic Gardens
Botanic Road, Glasnevin
Covering 19.5 hectares, these beautiful gardens contain a huge assortment of trees, plants and shrubs. Rare blooms and palms are housed in the huge Victorian conservatories.
Visiting Times:
Mon - Sat
9a.m. - 6p.m. in summer
10a.m. - 4.30p.m. in winter
Sundays
10a.m. - 6p.m. in summer
10a.m. - 4.30p.m. in winter
Closed Christmas day.
Alpine house closed Saturdays.
Admission Free   3 **A2**

Phoenix Park
North-western edge of city
Acknowledged as one of the largest enclosed urban parks in the world, it covers 1,760 acres, with a circumference of seven miles. Close to the main entrance at Parkgate Street are the Peoples Gardens and the Zoological Gardens (see separate entry). Within the park are the residence of the President of Ireland (Áras an Uachtaráin), the American Ambassador's residence and Ordnance Survey Ireland.
Visiting Times:
Phoenix Park is open to the public at all times but the Peoples Gardens have their own opening times.
Mon - Fri 7.30a.m - 9p.m.
Sat 10.30a.m. - 9p.m.
Sun 10a.m. - 9p.m.
NOTE: The Peoples Gardens will close at Dusk during Winter.
Admission Free   17 **B1**

Irish National War Memorial Park

St Anne's Park and Gardens
Mount Prospect Avenue, Clontarf
In a pleasant setting adjacent to Dollymount Strand, the rose gardens in this park cover over three acres alone. The Park and Gardens are open all year round. Admission free. Entrance Howth Road/All Saints Road.   **8 D2**

St Stephen's Green
Covering twenty-two acres at the top of Grafton Street, St Stephen's Green is right in the heart of the city. The varied landscaping of this delightful park includes trees, flower beds, a waterfall and an artificial lake. Several notable monuments and sculptures may also be seen.

Visiting Hours:
8 a.m. to Dusk Mon. - Sat.
10 a.m. to Dusk Sun. and Public Holidays
10 a.m. - 1 p.m Christmas Day
                                                28 C1

Zoological Gardens
Phoenix Park
In these outstanding attractive gardens may be seen a large collection of wild animals and birds from all over the world. Spacious houses and outdoor enclosures add to the total effect. Lion breeding has a long and distinguished history at Dublin Zoo. Two natural lakes house pelicans, flamingoes, ducks and geese.

Visiting Times:
Weekdays: 9.30a.m. - 6p.m.
Sundays 10.30a.m. - 6p.m.
Last admission 1 hour before closing
Gardens close at dusk in winter.   **9 A3**

The Peoples Gardens - Phoenix Park

Art Galleries

Hugh Lane Municipal Gallery of Modern Art
Charlemont House, Parnell Square
The building built between 1762 and 1765 was formerly the residence of Lord Charlemont. The gallery has an interesting collection of works by 19th and 20th century artists. Sir Hugh Lane who was drowned in the sinking of the Lusitania in 1915 contributed the nucleus of this collection of pictures.

Visiting Times:
Tues - Thurs 9.30a.m. - 6p.m.
Fri - Sat 9.30a.m. - 5p.m.
Sun 11a.m. - 5p.m.
Closed Monday
Admission Free   **12 C3**

National Gallery
Merrion Lawn, Merrion Square West
The gallery which contains over 2000 pictures, consisted of only 100 pictures when it was officially opened in 1864. As well as representing all the European schools, there is a comprehensive collection of works by Irish artists.
The Art Reference Library is open from Monday to Friday.

Visiting Times:
Mon to Sat 9.30a.m. - 5.30p.m.
Sun 12 noon - 5.30p.m.
Thurs open 9.30a.m. - 8.30p.m.
Free public lectures Sundays 3p.m. and Tuesdays 10.30a.m.
Conducted tours of Gallery on Sat. 3p.m. and Sun. at 2p.m., 3p.m. and 4p.m.
Closed on Good Friday and Dec. 24th - 26th.
Admission free.   **20 D3**

Museums

Dublin Civic Museum
South William Street
Occupying the former City Assembly House. It contains a permanent collection of exhibits of antiquarian and historical interest pertaining to Dublin City.
Visiting Times:
[June 2005] Closed until further notice. For information Tel. 6794260.

20 **C3**

Genealogical Office and Heraldic Museum
2 Kildare Street, Dublin 2.
The oldest office of state in Ireland founded in 1552. See the unique heraldic museum with its colourful display of coats of arms, banners and facility.
Avail of the Consultancy Service on ancestry tracing designed to enable you to undertake on your own the task of uncovering your Irish roots.
Visiting Hours:
Mon - Wed 10a.m. - 8.30p.m.
Thurs - Fri 10a.m. - 4.30p.m.
Saturday 10a.m. - 12.30p.m.   20 D3

Genealogical Office

Irish Jewish Museum
Walworth Road
Opened in 1985 by President Herzog of Israel who was educated in Dublin.
Housed in a restored synagogue with documents, photographs and memorabilia showing the history of Irish Jews dating back over 150 years.
Visiting Times:
May - Sept
Tues/Thurs/Sun 11a.m. - 3.30pm
Oct to April
Sunday Only 10.30a.m. - 2.30pm   27 **B2**

National Museum
Kildare Street
The museum houses one of the most impressive collection of antiques in Europe. Items displayed cover every age from the Stone Age to Medieval Times. Items of particular interest are the Tara Brooch, the Cross of Cong and the Ardagh Chalice. One of its most recent additions is the Derrynaflan Hoard which was found in a bog in Tipperary in 1980. The main entrance is from Kildare Street but part of the natural history division is approached from Merrion Street.
Visiting Times:
Tue - Sat 10a.m. - 5p.m.
Sun 2p.m. - 5p.m.
Closed Mondays, Christmas Day and Good Friday.   20 **D3**

National Wax Museum
On display are life-size figures of prominent Irish historical, political, theatrical, literary and sporting personalities. Taped narrations on each scene, guide one along.
Visiting Times:
The National Wax Museum is moving to Smithfield and will reopen Feb/Mar 2006.For more information Tel. 8722077

11 **B3**

The Writer's Museum
18/19 Parnell Square North
Opened in 1991 in two restored Georgian houses. It features a display of paintings, photographs, manuscripts and other memorabilia relating to Irish writers such as Shaw, Yeats, Beckett, Wilde, O'Casey, Joyce Behan and Swift
Visiting Times:
Mon - Sat 10a.m. - 5p.m.
Sun/Public Holiday 11.30a.m. - 5p.m.
June - August
Mon - Fri 10a.m. - 6p.m.
Closed 24th - 26th December   20 **C3**

Phoenix Park Visitor Centre
Phoenix Park

Located 5kms from the City Centre. The Tower House close to the visitor centre possibly dates from the 17th Century.

There are exhibitions, a film show and visitors can view a colourful and realistic interpretation of the past.

Visiting Times:
Nov - Mid March
10a.m. - 5p.m. Sat - Sun
Mid March - Late March
10a.m. - 5.30p.m. Daily
April - Sept
10a.m. - 6p.m. Daily
Oct 10a.m. - 5p.m. Daily
Last admission 45 minutes before closing. Free guided tours of Áras an Uachtaráin Saturdays only. Phone 6709155   9 **A3**

Dublinia - Christ Church
St Michael's Hill

The realistic and novel exhibition that is Dublinia is situated in the old Synod Hall on St Michael's Hill, alongside of Christ Church Cathedral, to which it is connected by an ornate pedistrian archway over St Michael's Hill.

The exhibition heralds the arrival of the Anglo-Normans in 1170 through a broad spectrum of Dublin life to the closure of the Monasteries in 1540.

Visiting Times:
April - September
10a.m. - 5p.m. Daily
October - March
11a.m. - 4p.m. (Mon. - Fri.)
10a.m. - 4p.m. (Sat/Sun/Bank Holiday)
Closed 24th - 26th December and 17th March   19 **B3**

Dunsink Observatory
Dunsink Lane, near Castleknock

Founded in 1783, this is one of the world's oldest observatories. It formerly belonged to Trinity College but is now the centre of the School of Astronomical Physics of the Dublin Institute for Advanced Studies.

Visiting Times:
Open to the public on the first and third Wednesday of each month from October to March, at 8p.m. Admission free on written application to the secretary enclosing stamp-addressed envelope. 9 **A1**

The James Joyce Centre
35 North Great Georges Street

The centre is housed in a beautifully restored 18th century Georgian Town-house only 300 metres from O'Connell Street. The aim of the centre is to promote an interest in the life and works of James Joyce and to this end there are daily talks, conducted tours of the house and walks through the heartland of Joyce's North inner city.

Visiting Times:
Mon. - Sat. 9.30a.m. - 5p.m.
Sun./Bank Holiday 12.30p.m. - 5p.m.
Closed 24th - 26th Dec, 1st Jan and Good Friday.   12 **C3**

Waterways Visitor Centre
Grand Canal Quay, Dublin 2

The centre houses an exhibition outlining the history of Ireland's inland waterways and the activities and experiences current-ly available.

Featuring an audio-visual show and work-ing models of various engineering fea-tures.

Visiting Times:
June - September
9.30a.m. - 5.30p.m. daily
Oct - May
Wed to Sun 12.30p.m. - 5.30p.m.
Last admission 45 minutes before closing.
21 **B3**

Waterways Visitor Centre

Christ Church Cathedral
Christchurch Place
Built in 1173 by Strongbow on a site originally occupied by a church built in 1030 by Sitric the Viking King. The present structure dates from the 19th century, although the medieval crypt still remains. It contains many interesting historical remains.
Visiting Times:
Mon - Fri 9.45a.m. - 4.30p.m.
Saturday 10a.m. - 4.30p.m.
Sunday 12.45p.m. - 2.45p.m.
Closed 26th December   19 **B3**

St Anne's Church
Dawson Street
Designed by Isaac Wells in neoroman-esque style in 1720. The facade was added by Sir Thomas Deane in 1868.
                              20 **D3**

St Audeon's Church
High Street.
St Audeon's dates from medieval times and is the oldest of Dublin's parish churches. The tower houses Ireland's three most ancient bells, dating from 1423. St Audeon's Arch stands nearby. This is Dublin's only surviving city gate.
Visiting Times:
June - Sep 9.30a.m. - 5.30p.m. Daily
Guided Tours every 30mins.
Last tour starts 4.45p.m.   19 **A3**

St Mary's Abbey
Meetinghouse Lane (off Capel St.)
The Abbey was founded in 1139 as a daughter house of the Benedictine Order of Savigny. It was one of the largest and most important monasteries in Ireland. The Chapter House is all that remains of the Abbey which houses an interesting historical exhibition.
Visiting Times:
Mid June - Mid Sept.
Wed and Sat only 10a.m. - 5p.m.
Last tour 45 minutes before closing.
                              19 **B2**

St Mary's Church
Mary Street
Dating from 1627, this was the first Dublin church to be built with galleries. Theobald Wolfe Tone was baptised here in 1763 and Sean O'Casey the playwright in 1880. This church is now a retail outlet   19 **B1**

St. Mary's Abbey

St Mary's Pro-Cathedral
Marlborough Street
Designed by John Sweetman and built between 1815 and 1825 in the Great Down Style. The Metropolitan Church of the diocese, it is used for state functions.
                              20 **C1**

St Michan's Church
Church Street
Founded by the Norse in 1096, the present building dates from 1685-6, having been much restored in 1828. The church's Harris organ is said to have been used by Handel during his visit to Dublin.
Vaults beneath the church contain mummified corpses which may be seen by the public.
Visiting Times:
Church and Vaults:
April - Oct.
Mon - Fri 10a.m. - 4.30p.m.
Closed 12.30p.m. - 2p.m.
Nov - March
Mon - Fri 12.30p.m. - 3.30p.m.
Saturday 10a.m. - 12.45p.m. (all year)
Vaults closed on Sunday   19 **A2**

St Patrick's Cathedral
Patrick Street

Built on the site of a 6th century church said to have been founded by St Patrick himself. The present church was commenced in 1191. In 1213 it gained Cathedral status. A university was established there in 1320 but was suppressed by Henry VIII. The square tower was built in the 14th century and houses the largest ringing bells in Ireland. Jonathan Swift was Dean of St Patrick's from 1713 to 1745.

Visiting Times:

Mon - Fri 9a.m. - 6p.m.

Sat **Mar - Oct** 9a.m. - 6p.m.

　　Nov - Feb 9a.m. - 5p.m.

Sun **Mar - Oct** 9a.m. - 11a.m., 12.45p.m. - 3p.m. and 4.15p.m. - 6p.m.

　　Nov - Feb 10a.m. - 11a.m. and 12.45p.m. - 3p.m.　　　**19 B3**

St Werburgh's Church
Werburgh Street

Erected in 1715 on the site of the medieval successor to pre Norman St Werburgh's. Destroyed by fire in 1754, the church was re-opened in 1759. In the vaults beneath the church is buried Lord Edward Fitzgerald.

Visiting Times:

By appointment only.

Tel: 4783710

Mon - Fri 10a.m. - 4p.m.

Sunday Service 10a.m.　　　**19 B3**

University Church
St Stephen's Green

Founded by Cardinal Newman, it was designed in a neo-Byzantine style by John Hungerford Pollen. It was built between 1854 and 1856.

28 C1

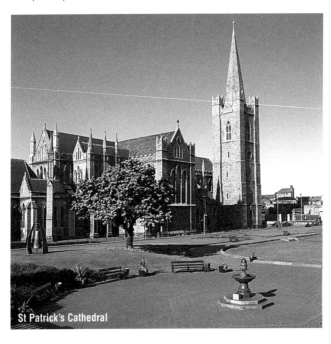

St Patrick's Cathedral

Libraries

Chester Beatty Library
Dublin Castle

On of the world's most valuable private collections of oriental manuscripts and miniatures can be seen here. There are manuscripts of the New Testament, Manichean papyri and Eastern miniatures, as well as picture scrolls, albums and jades from the Far East. The library is located in the Clock Tower building.

Visiting Times:
May - Sept
Mon - Fri 10a.m. - 5p.m.
Oct - April
Tue - Fri 10a.m. - 5p.m.
Saturday 11a.m. - 5p.m. (all year)
Sunday 1p.m. - 5p.m. (all year)
Closed Public Holiday Monday's, Good Friday, 24th - 26th Dec and 1st Jan. 19 **B3**

Marsh's Library
St Patrick's Close

This is Ireland's oldest public library, founded in 1701 by Archbishop Narcissus Marsh. The collection consists mainly of theological, medical, ancient historical, Hebrew, Syriac, Greek, French and Latin literature.

Visiting Hours:
Mon - Fri 10a.m. - 5p.m.
Closed 1p.m. - 2p.m.
Saturday 10.30a.m. - 1p.m.
Closed Tuesday, Sunday and Bank Holidays   27 **B1**

National Library
Kildare Street

Founded in 1877 this is Ireland's largest public library. It contains over half a million books as well as maps, prints and manuscripts. It also houses a large newspaper collection.

Visiting Times:
Mon - Wed (incl) 10a.m. - 9p.m.
Thurs/Fri 10a.m. - 5p.m.
Saturday 10a.m. to 1p.m.   20 **D3**

Royal Irish Academy Library
19 Dawson Street

One of the most extensive collections of ancient Irish manuscripts can be seen here. These include the *Book of the Dun Cow* the *Book of Ballymote*, the *Speckled Book*, the *Slowe Missal* and the *Cathac* or *Battle Book* reputed to be the actual copy of the Psalms made in the 6th century by St Colmcille.

Visiting Times:
Mon - Thur 9.30a.m. - 5.30p.m.
Friday 9.30a.m. - 5p.m.
Closes 5p.m. during **August**
Closed Public Holidays.   20 **D3**

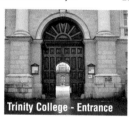

Trinity College - Entrance

Trinity College Library
College Green

Dating from the late sixteenth century, Trinity College Library is Ireland's oldest library. It contains over 1,000,000 volumes and Ireland's most extensive collection of manuscripts and early printed books. Its greatest treasure is the Book of Kells (probably eight century).
The library is housed in two buildings - the Old Library (completed in 1732) and the New Library (1967).

Visiting Times:
Mon - Sat 9.30a.m. - 5p.m.
May - Sept
Sunday 9.30a.m. - 4.30p.m.
Public Holiday 9.30a.m. -5p.m.
Oct - April
Sunday 12noon - 4.30p.m.
Public Holiday 12.30p.m. - 4.30p.m.
                                       20 **D2**

STREET INDEX

Street Name	Page/Grid Ref.
Abbey Cottages	20 C2²
Abbey Court	7 B1
Abbey Park	7 B1
Abbey Street Lr	20 D1
Abbey Street Mid	20 C2
Abbey Street Old	20 D1
Abbey Street Upr	19 B2
Abbeyfield	8 C1
Abercorn Road	21 B1
Aberdeen Street	18 C1
Achill Road	4 D2
Adair	30 D3⁴
Adair Lane	20 C2³
Addison Drive	3 A1
Addison Lane	3 A1
Addison Place	3 B2
Addison Road	13 B1
Adelaide Court	28 C2
Adelaide Road	28 C2
Adelaide Terrace	25 B1
Aikenhead Terrace	22 D3
Albert Court	21 B3
Albert Place East	21 B3⁸
Albert Place West	28 C2
Albert Terrace	28 C2¹¹
Aldborough Parade	13 A3
Aldborough Place	13 A3
Aldborough Square	13 A3¹²
Alexandra Quay	22 D2²
Alexandra Quay (Apts)	23 A1
Alexandra Road	23 A1
Alexandra Rd Ext	24 D1
Alexandra Terrace (North Wall)	22 C1
Alexandra Terrace	27 B2
Alfie Byrne Road	14 C2
All Hallow's Gardens	4 D2
Allingham Street	26 D1
Almeida Avenue	17 B3⁸
Almeida Terrace	25 B1¹
Alverno	15 B2¹
Amiens Street	13 A3
Anglesea Road	30 C3
Anglesea Row	19 B1
Anglesea Street	20 C2
Annadale Avenue	5 B3
Annadale Crescent	5 B2
Annadale Drive	5 B2
Annaly Road	10 D1
Annamoe Drive	10 D2
Annamoe Parade	10 D2
Annamoe Park	10 D2
Annamoe Road	10 C2
Annamoe Terrace	10 D2
Anne Street North	19 B1
Anne Street South	20 C3
Anne's Lane	20 C3
Anner Road	25 A1
Annesley Avenue	13 B2²
Annesley Bridge Rd	13 B2
Annesley Place	13 B2
Aranmore Avenue	11 B2⁷
Arbour Hill	18 C1
Arbour Place	18 D1
Arbour Terrace	18 C1
Arbutus Avenue	27 A3
Arbutus Place	27 B2
Ard Righ Place	18 D1
Ard Righ Road	18 D1
Ardagh Road	25 B3
Ardee Grove	27 B3
Ardee Road	28 C3
Ardee Row	27 A1
Ardee Street	27 A1
Ardilaun Road	13 A2
Ardmore Avenue	10 C2
Ardoyne House	29 B3³
Ardpatrick Road	9 A1
Argyle Road	29 B3
Arklow Street	10 C3
Armstrong Street	27 A3³
Army Road	17 A1
Arnott Street	27 B1
Arran Quay	19 A2
Arran Quay Terrace	19 A2
Arran Road	4 D2
Arran Street East	19 B2
Arran Street West	19 A2
Asdill's Row	20 C2⁵
Ash Grove	19 A3¹⁴
Ash Street	19 A3
Ashbrook	7 A3
Ashford Cottages	10 C3²
Ashford Place	10 C3¹
Ashford Street	10 C3
Ashington Court	1 A2
Ashington Mews	1 A2
Ashling Close	8 B3
Ashmount Court	17 A3⁸
Ashworth Place	27 B3³
Aston Place	20 C2
Aston Quay	20 C2
Athlumney Villas	28 C3
Auburn	7 A3
Auburn Street	11 B3
Auburn Terrace	17 B3¹⁰
Auburn Walk	10 C3
Aughavanagh Rd	26 D3
Aughrim Court	10 D3⁴
Aughrim Lane	10 D3
Aughrim Place	10 D3
Aughrim Street	10 C3
Aughrim Villas	10 D3¹
Aungier Lane	28 C1¹
Aungier Place	28 C1
Aungier Street	20 C3
Austin's Cottages	13 B2¹⁰
Ave Maria Road	26 C1
Avenue Road	27 B2
Avondale Avenue	11 A2
Avondale House	12 D3¹⁹
Avondale Road	11 A2
Bachelor's Walk	20 C2
Bachelor's Way	20 C2
Back Lane	19 B3
Baggot Close	28 D1
Baggot Court	29 A1
Baggot Street Lwr	29 A1
Baggot Street Upr	29 A2
Baggotrath Place	29 A1²
Bailey's Row	13 A3
Balfe Street	20 C3³
Ball's Lane	19 B1
Ballsbridge	30 C3
Ballsbridge Avenue	30 C3
Ballsbridge Gardens	30 C2
Ballsbridge Park	30 D3⁶
Ballsbridge Terrace	30 C3¹
Ballsbridge Wood	30 C2
Ballyboggan Road	1 A1
Ballybough Avenue	13 A2¹⁵
Ballybough Court	13 A2¹⁴
Ballybough Lane	13 A2¹²
Ballybough Road	13 A2
Ballygall Road East	3 A1
Ballymun Road	3 B1
Bangor Drive	25 B3
Bangor Road	25 B3
Bann Road	2 C2
Bannaville	28 C3⁴
Bannow Road	1 B2
Bantry Road	4 C1
Bargy Road	14 C3
Barnamore Grove	1 A1
Barnamore Park	1 A1
Barrack Lane	30 D1³
Barrow Place	4 C2
Barrow Road	2 C2

Barrow Street	22 C3	
Basin Street Lwr	18 C3	
Basin Street Upr	18 C3	
Bass Place	21 A3	
Bath Avenue	30 C1	
Bath Ave Gdns	30 C1	
Bath Avenue Place	30 C1	
Bath Lane	12 C3	
Bath Street	22 D3	
Bayview Avenue	13 A2	
Beach Avenue	31 A1	
Beach Drive	31 A1	
Beach Road	31 A1	
Beatty's Avenue	30 C2	
Beaucourt	4 D2[1]	
Beaver Close	13 A3[9]	
Beaver Street	13 A3	
Bective Square	11 B2[11]	
Bedford Lane	20 C2	
Bedford Row	20 C2[4]	
Beggars Bush Court	30 C1[6]	
Belgrove Park	8 D3	
Belgrove Road	16 D1	
Bell's Lane	28 D1	
Bella Avenue	12 D3[7]	
Bella Place	12 D3[6]	
Bella Street	12 D3	
Bellevue	18 D3	
Bellevue Cottages	2 D1[1]	
Bellevue Maltings	17 A2	
Bellman's Walk	21 B1[4]	
Belmont Place	12 D3[16]	
Belton Park Avenue	6 D1	
Belton Park Gardens	6 D1	
Belton Park Road	6 D1	
Belton Park Villas	6 D2	
Belvidere Avenue	12 D2[5]	
Belvidere Court	12 C2	
Belvidere Place	12 D2	
Belvidere Road	12 C2	
Ben Edar Road	10 C3	
Benbulbin Avenue	25 A2	
Benbulbin Rd	25 A2	
Benburb Street	18 D2	
Bengal Terrace	3 A3	
Benson Street	22 C2	
Beresford Avenue	5 A2	
Beresford Green	5 A2	
Beresford Lawn	5 A2	
Beresford Place	20 D1	
Beresford Street	19 B1	
Berkeley Avenue	11 B2	
Berkeley Mews	30 C1[5]	
Berkeley Place	11 B2	
Berkeley Road	11 B2	
Berkeley Street	11 B2	
Berkeley Terrace	30 C1	
Berystede	29 A3[2]	
Bessborough Ave	13 B2	
Bessborough Pde	28 C3	
Bethany House	31 B3[1]	
Bethesda Place	12 C3[8]	
Beverly Court	8 D3	
Bishop Street	27 B1	
Black Street	17 B1[2]	
Blackberry Lane	28 C3	
Blackhall Green	18 D1	
Blackhall Parade	19 A1	
Blackhall Place	18 D2	
Blackhall Street	19 A1	
Blackheath Avenue	8 C3	
Blackheath Court	8 D3	
Blackheath Drive	8 C3	
Blackheath Gardens	8 C3	
Blackheath Grove	8 C3	
Blackheath Park	8 C3	
Blackhorse Avenue	9 A2	
Blackhorse Grove	10 C3	
Blackpitts	27 A1	
Blackwater Road	2 C2	
Blessington Court	11 B3[7]	
Blessington Lane	11 B3	
Blessington Place	11 B2[13]	
Blessington Street	11 B3	
Bloomfield Avenue	27 B2	
Bloomfield Avenue (Ranelagh)	29 A3	
Bloomfield Cottages	27 B2[6]	
Bloomfield Park	27 B2	
Blythe Avenue	21 B1[2]	
Boardman's Lane	26 C1[5]	
Bond Drive	15 A3	
Bond Road	14 D3	
Bond Street	18 D3	
Bonham Street	18 D2	
Boolavogue Road	14 C3[1]	
Borris Court	19 B3[5]	
Botanic Avenue	4 C3	
Botanic Hall	3 A1	
Botanic Park	4 C3	
Botanic Road	3 B3	
Botanic Villas	3 B3	
Boundary Road	14 D2	
Bow Bridge	18 C3	
Bow Lane East	20 C3	
Bow Lane West	18 C3	
Bow Street	19 A1	
Boyne Lane	21 A3	
Boyne Road	1 B2	
Boyne Street	21 A3	
Brabazon Place	27 A1[8]	
Brabazon Row	27 A1	
Brabazon Square	19 A3[3]	
Brabazon Street	19 A3[7]	
Bracken's Lane	20 D2[3]	
Brainsboro Terrace	27 A2[4]	
Braithwaite Street	18 D3	
1 Branch Rd N	23 A1	
1 Branch Rd S	23 A1	
2 Branch Rd N	23 B1	
2 Branch Rd S	23 A1	
3 Branch Rd S	23 A1	
4 Branch Rd S	23 B1	
Brandon Terrace	26 D1[4]	
Breakwater Rd Nth	24 C1	
Breakwater Rd Sth	24 C1	
Bregia Road	10 D1	
Bremen Avenue	23 A3	
Bremen Grove	23 A3	
Bremen Road	23 A3	
Brenden Barna Ct	12 D2[16]	
Brian Avenue	6 C3	
Brian Boru Avenue	16 D2	
Brian Boru Street	16 D2	
Brian Road	6 C3/13 B1	
Brian Terrace	13 B1	
Brickfield Drive	25 B2	
Brickfield Lane	26 D1	
Bride Close	19 B2[17]	
Bride Court	19 B3[17]	
Bride Road	19 B3	
Bride Street	19 B3	
Bridge Court	29 B1[8]	
Bridge Street	22 D3	
Bridge Street Lower	19 A2	
Bridge Street Upper	19 A3	
Bridgefoot Street	19 A2	
Bridgewater Quay	17 A2	
Brighton Avenue	6 D3	
Britain Place	12 C3[10]	
Britain Quay	22 C2	
Broadstone Avenue	11 B3[12]	
Brodin Row	18 C1	
Brookfield Road	17 B3	
Brookfield Street	25 B1	
Brooklawn	15 A1	
Brookwood Ave	8 D1	
Brookwood Glen	8 D1	
Brookwood Meadow	8 C1	
Brookwood Park	8 C1	
Brookwood Rise	8 D1	
Broombridge Road	1 B2	
Brown Street North	19 A1	
Brown Street South	26 D1	
Brunswick Place	21 B3	

Brunswick St Nth	19 A1
Brunswick Villas	20 D2[4]
Buckingham Place	13 A3[6]
Buckingham St Lwr	13 A3
Buckingham St Upr	13 A3
Buckingham Village	12 D3[12]
Bulfin Gardens	17 A3
Bulfin Road	25 A1
Bull Alley Street	19 B3
Burgess Lane	19 A2[1]
Burgh Quay	20 D2
Burke Place	18 C3
Burleigh Court	29 A2
Burlington Gardens	29 A2
Burlington Road	29 A2
Byrne's Lane	20 C2
Cabra	10 C1
Cabra Drive	10 C2
Cabra Grove	10 C2
Cabra Park	11 A1
Cabra Road	10 C2
Cadogan Road	13 B1
Calderwood Avenue	5 B1
Calderwood Grove	5 B2
Calderwood Road	5 B1
Caledon Road	14 C3
Camac Terrace	17 B3[16]
Cambridge Avenue	23 A3
Cambridge Court	22 D3[1]
Cambridge Park	22 D3
Cambridge Road	22 D3
Cambridge Square	22 D2[3]
Cambridge Street	22 D2
Cambridge Terrace	28 D3
Camden Buildings	28 C1[6]
Camden Court	28 C2[1]
Camden Lock	22 C3
Camden Market	28 C2[3]
Camden Place	28 C1
Camden Row	27 B1
Camden St Lwr	28 C1
Camden St Old	28 C2[2]
Camden St Upr	28 C2
Camden Villas	28 C1[5]
Cameron Square	17 B3
Cameron Street	26 D1
Camogie Road	17 A1
Campbell's Court	19 B1
Campbell's Lane	12 D2[6]
Campbell's Row	12 D2[7]
Canal Road	28 C3
Canon Lillis Avenue	13 B3
Canon Mews East	30 C1[9]
Canon Mooney Gdns	22 D3[2]
Caragh Court	13 B1[1]

Caragh Road	9 B2
Carberry Road	5 B1
Carbury Terrace	22 C1[1]
Cardiff Lane	21 B2
Cards Lane	20 D2[5]
Carleton Road	6 C3
Carlingford Parade	21 B2
Carlingford Road	4 C3
Carlisle Street	27 B2
Carlton Court	15 A1
Carlton Villas	30 C2[3]
Carman's Hall	19 A3
Carnew Street	10 C3
Carnlough Road	1 B3/10 C1
Caroline Row	22 D3
Carrick Terrace	26 C1
Carrickfoyle Tce	17 A3[5]
Carrigallen Drive	1 B1
Carrigallen Park	1 B1
Carrigallen Road	1 B1
Casino Park	6 D2
Casino Road	5 B3
Castilla Park	8 D3
Castle Avenue	8 C3/15 B1
Castle Court	7 A3
Castle Grove	7 B3
Castle Market	20 C3
Castle Road	16 C1
Castle Street	19 B3
Castle Terrace	11 A2[1]
Castleforbes Road	22 C1
Cathal Brugha St	20 C1
Cathedral Lane	27 B1
Cathedral Street	20 C1
Cathedral View Ct	27 B1
Cathedral View Wk	27 B1[5]
Catherine Court	13 A3
Catherine Lane N	19 A1[3]
Catherine Street	19 A3
Cavendish Row	12 C3[9]
Ceannt Fort	17 B3[9]
Cecil Avenue	6 D3
Cecilia Street	20 C2[8]
Celestine Avenue	22 D3
Celtic Park Avenue	6 D1
Celtic Park Road	6 C1
Chamber Street	27 A1
Champion's Avenue	20 D1
Champion Quay	20 C2[11]
Chancery Lane	19 B3
Chancery Place	19 B2
Chancery Street	19 B2
Chapel Avenue	22 D3
Chapel Lane	19 B1
Charlemont	6 C1

Charlemont Grdns	28 C2[7]
Charlemont Mall	28 C2
Charlemont Parade	13 A2[8]
Charlemont Place	28 C2[14]
Charlemont Place	28 D2
Charlemont Road	6 D3
Charlemont Street	28 C2
Charles Lane	12 D2
Charles St Gt	12 D3
Charles St W	19 B2
Charleville Avenue	13 A2
Charleville Mall	13 A2
Charleville Road	10 D2
Charlotte Quay	22 C3
Charlotte Way	28 C2
Chatham Court	20 C3[14]
Chatham Lane	20 C3[2]
Chatham Row	20 C3[5]
Chatham Street	20 C3
Chelmsford Avenue	28 D3
Chelmsford Road	29 A3
Chelsea Gardens	16 D1
Cheltenham Place	28 C3[3]
Cherrymount Cres	6 D2[3]
Cherrymount Grove	6 D2[2]
Cherrymount Park	11 A2
Chesterfield Avenue	17 A1
Christchurch Place	19 B3
Christchurch Sq	19 B3[9]
Church Avenue	3 B1
Church Avenue (Drumcondra)	4 D2
Church Avenue (East Wall)	22 C1[4]
Church Avenue (Irishtown)	30 D1
Church Ave S	26 C1
Church Ave W	19 A1
Church Lane	4 D2
Church Lane	20 C2
Church Lane South	27 B1[6]
Church Place	22 C1[3]
Church Road	13 B3
Church Road	14 C3
Church Row	22 C1[5]
Church Street	19 A2
Church St East	22 C1
Church St New	19 A2
Church St Upr	19 A1
Church Terrace	19 A1
Church View	4 D2
Churchgate Avenue	16 D2[1]
Churchill Terrace	30 D3[5]
Cian Park	4 D3
City Quay	21 A2

Clanawley Road	7 B2	
Clanboy Road	7 B1	
Clanbrassil Close	27 A2	
Clanbrassil St Lwr	27 A2	
Clanbrassil St Upr	27 A2	
Clancarthy Road	7 A2	
Clandonagh Road	7 A1	
Clanhugh Road	7 B2	
Clanmahon Road	7 B1	
Clanmaurice Road	7 A1	
Clanmoyle Road	7 A2	
Clanranald Road	7 A1	
Clanree Road	7 A1	
Clanwilliam Court	29 B1[6]	
Clanwilliam Place	29 B1	
Clanwilliam Square	21 B3[5]	
Clanwilliam Terrace	21 B3[6]	
Clare Lane	20 D3	
Clare Park Villas	4 D1	
Clare Road	4 D1	
Clare Street	20 D3	
Claremont Avenue	3 B1	
Claremont Close	31 A2[5]	
Claremont Close	2 D3	
Claremont Court (Glasnevin)	2 D2	
Claremont Court (Sandymount)	30 D2[4]	
Claremont Crescent	2 D2	
Claremont Lawns	3 A3	
Claremont Park	31 A2	
Claremont Road	31 A2	
Clarence Mangan Rd	27 A1	
Clarence Mangan Sq	19 B3[16]	
Clarence Pl Gt	21 B3	
Clarence St Gt N	13 A3	
Clarendon Market	20 C3[6]	
Clarendon Row	20 C3[13]	
Clarendon Street	20 C3	
Clareville Court	3 A3	
Clareville Grove	3 A3	
Clarke's Terrace	26 C1	
Claude Road	11 B1	
Cliftonville Road	3 B3	
Clinch's Court	13 A2[6]	
Clogher Road	26 C3	
Cloister Court	1 A2[1]	
Clonard Road	25 A3	
Clonlara Road	23 A3	
Clonliffe Avenue	13 A2	
Clonliffe Gardens	13 A1	
Clonliffe Road	12 D1/13 A1	
Clonmel Street	28 C1	
Clonmore Court	3 B1	
Clonmore Road	13 A2	
Clonmore Terrace	13 A2	
Clonmore Villas	13 A2[4]	
Clontarf Park	16 D2	
Clontarf Road	14 D1/16 D2	
Clontarf Avenue	4 D2	
Clonturk Gardens	4 D3[2]	
Clonturk Park	4 D3	
Cloonlara Crescent	1 B1	
Clyde Lane	29 B3	
Clyde Road	29 B3	
Coburg Street	13 A3	
Cois Eala	27 B3	
Coke Lane	19 A2[2]	
Coke Ovens Cotts	2 D3[1]	
Colbert's Fort	26 C1[2]	
Coleraine Street	19 B1	
College Green	20 C2	
College Lane	21 A3[4]	
College Street	20 D2	
Collins Avenue	6 C1	
Collins Avenue East	7 A2	
Collins Court	6 C1	
Collins Park	6 D1	
Commons Street	21 A1	
Comyn Place	4 C2	
Con Colbert Road	17 A3	
Connaught Parade	11 A1[1]	
Connaught Street	11 A1	
Conquer Hill Ave	16 D2	
Constitution Hill	11 B3	
Constitution Hill (Flats)	19 B1[3]	
Convent Avenue	13 A1	
Convent Close	29 A1[1]	
Convent Place	28 D2[1]	
Convent View Cotts	1 A3	
Convent View Cres	1 A3	
Conway Court	21 B3[9]	
Conyngham Road	17 B2	
Cook Street	19 A2	
Coolevin Road	27 B1	
Coombe Court	19 A3[8]	
Cope Street	20 C2	
Copeland Avenue	6 D3	
Copeland Grove	6 D3	
Copper Alley	19 B2	
Coppinger Row	20 C3[4]	
Cork Hill	19 B2[8]	
Cork Street	26 D1	
Corn Exchange Pl	20 D2[1]	
Cornmarket	19 A3	
Countess Markievicz House	21 A2[5]	
Courtney Place	13 B2[1]	
Cow Parlour	27 A1[4]	
Cowper Street	10 C3	
Craigford Avenue	7 B1	
Craigford Drive	7 B1	
Crampton Court	20 C2[9]	
Crane Lane	19 B2	
Crane Street	18 D3	
Cranfield Place	31 A1	
Cranmer Lane	29 B1[1]	
Crawford Avenue	4 C3	
Creeg Court	20 C1	
Creighton Street	21 A2	
Cremore Avenue	3 A1	
Cremore Crescent	3 A1	
Cremore Drive	3 A1	
Cremore Lawn	2 D1	
Cremore Park	3 A1	
Cremore Road	3 A1	
Cremore Villas	3 A1	
Crescent Gardens	13 B2	
Crescent House	14 D1[1]	
Crescent Place	6 D3	
Crescent Villas	4 C3	
Crinan Strand	21 A1	
Croagh Patrick Rd	9 A1	
Cromwell's Quarters	18 C3	
Crosbie House	28 D3[5]	
Cross Kevin Street	27 B1[8]	
Crostick Alley	19 A3[15]	
Crow Street	20 C2	
Crown Alley	20 C2	
Croydon Gardens	5 B3	
Croydon Green	5 B3	
Croydon Pk Ave	6 C3	
Croydon Terrace	5 B3	
Crumlin Road	25 A3	
Cuala Road	10 D1	
Cuckoo Lane	19 B1	
Cuffe Lane	28 C1	
Cuffe Street	28 C1	
Cullen's Wood	28 D3[7]	
Cumberland Court	21 A3[3]	
Cumberland Road	29 A2	
Cumberland St Nth	12 D3	
Cumberland St Sth	21 A3	
Curved Street	20 C2[14]	
Curzon Street	27 B2	
Custom Hall	20 D1[9]	
Custom Ho. Quay	20 D1	
Cymbric Road	23 A3	
Dakota Court	11 B1	
Dalcassian Downs	11 A1	
Dalymount	11 A2	
Dame Court	20 C2	
Dame Lane	20 C2	
Dame Street	20 C2	
Danesfort	15 B2	

Daneswell Road	3	B3
Daniel Street	27	B1
Dargle Road	4	C3
Darley Street	27	A3
Darley's Terrace	26	D1
Dartmouth Lane	28	D3
Dartmouth Place	28	D3
Dartmouth Road	28	D3
Dartmouth Sq E	28	D3
Dartmouth Sq N	28	D2
Dartmouth Sq Sth	28	D3
Dartmouth Sq W	28	D3
Dartmouth Terrace	28	D3
David Park	11	B1
David Road	11	B1
Davis Place	19	B3[2]
Davitt Road	25	A1
Dawson Lane	20	D3
Dawson Street	20	D3
De Burgh Road	18	C2[1]
De Courcy Square	3	B3
De Valera Place	12	C2[9]
Dean Street	27	B1
Dean Swift Square	19	A3
Delvin Road	10	D1
Delvin Terrace	11	B3[16]
Demesne	8	C2
Denmark St Great	12	C3
Denzille Lane	21	A3
Dermot O'Hurley Ave	22	D3
Derrynane Gardens	22	D3
Derrynane Parade	12	C2[3]
Desmond Street	27	B2
Deverell Place	20	D1[6]
Devery's Lane	11	B1
Devlin's Place	21	A3
Devoy Road	25	A1
Dexter Terrace	28	D3[1]
Digges Lane	20	C3
Digges St Upr	28	C1
Dillon Place South	19	B3
Dingle Road	9	B1
Distillery Road	13	A1
Dodder Terrace	22	D3
Dodder View Cotts	30	C2[5]
D'Olier Street	20	D2
Dolphin Avenue	26	D2
Dolphin House	26	D2
Dolphin Park	25	B2
Dolphin Road	25	B2
Dolphin's Barn	26	C2
Dolphin's Barn St	26	C2
Dominick Lane	19	B1
Dominick Place	20	C1
Dominick St Upr	11	B3
Donelan Avenue	18	C3
Donnycarney	6	D1
Donnycarney Road	6	D2
Donore Avenue	26	D1
Donore Road	26	D1
Donore Terrace	26	D1
Donovan Lane	27	A2
Doon Avenue	10	C2
Doris Street	22	C3
Dorset Lane	12	C2
Dorset Place	12	C2
Dorset Street Lwr	12	C2
Dorset Street Upr	11	B3
Dowling's Court	21	A2
Downpatrick Road	25	B3
Dowth Avenue	10	D1
Dromard Terrace	31	A1
Drumalee Avenue	10	C3
Drumalee Court	10	C3
Drumalee Drive	10	C3
Drumalee Grove	10	C3
Drumalee Park	10	C3
Drumalee Road	10	C3
Drumcliffe Drive	10	C1
Drumcliffe Road	9	B1
Drumcondra	4	D2
Drumcondra Park	12	D2[1]
Drumcondra Rd Lwr	4	D3/12	C1
Drumcondra Rd Upr	4	D3
Drummond Place	27	B3[4]
Drury Street	20	C3
Duck Lane	19	A1
Dufferin Avenue	27	A2
Duke Lane Lower	20	C3
Duke Lane Upper	20	C3
Duke Row	13	A3[4]
Duke Street	20	C3
Dunard Avenue	9	A2
Dunard Court	9	B2
Dunard Drive	9	B2
Dunard Park	9	B2
Dunard Road	9	B2
Dunard Walk	9	B2
Duncan Court	8	D3[1]
Dunluce Road	8	C2
Dunmanus Road	1	B3
Dunne Street	13	A3
Dunseverick Road	7	B3
Durham Road	31	B2
Earl Place	20	C1
Earl Street North	20	C1
Earl Street South	19	A3
Earls Court	9	B2
East Point Business Park	14	D2
East Road	22	C1
East Road (East Wall)	14	C3
East Wall	14	C3
East Wall Road	14	C2
East Wall Rd (North Wall)	22	D1
Eastmoreland La	29	B2
Eastmoreland Pl	29	B2[1]
Ebenezer Terrace	26	C1
Eblana Villas	21	B3
Eccles Court	12	C2
Eccles Place	12	C2
Eccles Street	11	B2
Echlin Street	18	D3
Eden Quay	20	D2
Eden Terrace	4	C3
Edgewood	4	D3[1]
Elgin Road	29	B2
Elizabeth Street	12	D1
Ellesmere Avenue	10	C2
Ellford Terrace	26	D2[3]
Ellis Court	18	D2[6]
Ellis Quay	18	D2
Ellis Street	18	D2
Elm Mount Avenue	6	D1
Elm Mount Court	7	A1
Elm Mount Drive	7	A1
Elm Mount Road	7	A1
Elm Road	6	D1
Ely Place	28	D1
Ely Place Upper	28	D1[2]
Emerald Cottages	30	C1[2]
Emerald Place	21	A1
Emerald Square	26	C1
Emerald Street	21	B1
Emerald Terrace	26	D1
Emmet Road	17	A3
Emmet Street (Inchicore)	12	D2
Emmet Street (Harold's Cross)	27	A3
Emor Street	27	B2
Emorville Avenue	27	B2
Empress Place	13	A3
Engine Alley	19	A3[17]
Ennafort Court	8	D1
Ennafort Park	8	D1
Ennafort Road	8	D1
Ennaville Road	13	B2
Ennis Grove	30	D1
Enniskerry Road	11	B1

Erne Place Little	21 A3	
Erne Place Lower	21 A2	
Erne Street Lower	21 A2	
Erne Street Upper	21 A3	
Erne Terrace Front	21 A3	
Erne Terrace Rere	21 A3	
Erris Road	10 C1	
Esmond Avenue	13 B1	
Essex Gate	19 B2[1]	
Essex Quay	19 B2	
Essex Street E	20 C2	
Essex Street W	19 B2	
Estate Cottages	29 B1	
Estate Cottages	30 C2[6]	
(Ballsbridge)		
Eugene Street	26 D1	
Eustace Street	20 C2	
Everton Avenue	10 C2	
Ewington Lane	18 C3	
Exchange Street Lwr	19 B2	
Exchange Street Upr	19 B2[2]	
Exchequer Street	20 C3	
Fade Street	20 C3	
Fairfield Avenue	13 B3	
Fairfield Road	3 B3	
Fairview	14 C1	
Fairview Ave Lwr	13 B1	
Fairview Ave Upr	14 C1	
Fairview Green	13 B1	
Fairview Passage	13 B1	
Fairview Strand	13 B1	
Fairview Terrace	13 B1	
Faith Avenue	13 B2	
Farney Park	31 A2	
Father Matthew Sq	19 A1[4]	
Father Scully Hse	12 D3[17]	
Fatima Mansions	26 C1[3]	
Faussagh Avenue	1 B3	
Faussagh Road	10 D1	
Fenian Street	21 A3	
Ferguson Road	4 C2	
Fernley Court	27 B1	
Ferrymans Crossing	21 B1[3]	
Fertullagh Road	10 D1[1]	
Findlater Place	20 C1[1]	
Findlater Street	18 C1	
Fingal Place	10 D3	
Finglas Road	2 D2	
Finglas Road Old	2 D1	
Finglas Street	26 D1	
Finn Street	18 C1	
First Avenue	21 B1	
Fishamble Street	19 B2	
Fisherman's Wharf	22 D2[1]	
Fitzgerald Street	27 B3[2]	
Fitzgibbon Lane	12 D2	
Fitzgibbon Street	12 D2	
Fitzroy Avenue	12 D1	
Fitzwilliam Court	28 D1[1]	
Fitzwilliam Lane	29 A1	
Fitzwilliam Place	28 D2	
Fitzwilliam Pl Little	29 A1[3]	
Fitzwilliam Pl Nth	11 A1[1]	
Fitzwilliam Quay	22 D3	
Fitzwilliam Sq E	29 A1	
Fitzwilliam Sq N	29 A1	
Fitzwilliam Sq S	28 D1	
Fitzwilliam Sq W	28 D1	
Fitzwilliam Street	22 D3	
Fitzwilliam St. Lwr	29 A1	
Fitzwilliam St. Upr.	29 A1	
Flag Alley	19 A3[16]	
Fleet Street	20 C2	
Fleming Road	4 C2	
Fleming's Place	29 A2	
Florence Street	27 B2[4]	
Foley Street	20 D1	
Fontenoy Street	11 B3	
Forbes Lane	26 D1	
Forbes Street	21 B2	
Fort Ostman	25 B3	
Fortescue Lane	28 C3	
Forth Road	14 C3	
Fortview Avenue	16 D2[11]	
Foster Place North	13 A2	
Foster Place South	20 C2	
Foster Terrace	13 A2	
Fountain Place	19 A1	
Fountain Road	17 B1	
Fourth Avenue	21 B1	
Fownes St Lwr	20 C2[7]	
Fownes St Upr	20 C2	
Foyle Road	5 B3	
Francis Street	19 A3	
Frankfort Cottages	13 A3	
Frederick Court	12 C3[4]	
Frederick Lane N	12 C3[7]	
Frederick Lane S	20 D3	
Frederick St Nth	12 C3	
Frederick St Sth	20 D3	
French Mullen Flats	28 C2[8]	
Frenchman's Lane	20 D1[1]	
Friary Avenue	19 A1	
Friary Grove	19 A1[7]	
Fumbally Lane	27 B1	
Furry Park Court	8 C2	
Furry Park Road	8 C2	
Gaelic Street	13 B3	
Galmoy Road	10 D1	
Galtymore Drive	25 A2	
Galtymore Road	25 A2	
Gandon Hall	20 D1[8]	
Garda Terrace	18 C1	
Garden Lane	19 A3	
Garden Terrace	27 A2[6]	
Garden View	28 C3[5]	
Gardiner Lane	12 D3	
Gardiner Place	12 C3	
Gardiner Row	12 C3[5]	
Gardiner St Lwr	20 D1	
Gardiner St Mid	12 D3	
Gardiner St Upr	12 C2	
Gartan Avenue	12 C1	
Geoffrey Keating Rd	27 A1[3]	
George Reynolds Flats	22 D3[17]	
George's Hill	19 B1	
George's Lane	19 A1	
George's Place	12 C2[12]	
George's Quay	20 D2	
George's St Gt N	12 C3	
George's St Gt S	20 C3	
George's Wharf	11 B2[12]	
Gerald Street	22 C3	
Geraldine Street	11 B2	
Gilbert Road	27 A2	
Gilford Avenue	31 B3	
Gilford Court	31 A2	
Gilford Drive	31 A3	
Gilford Park	31 A3	
Gilford Road	31 A2	
Gilford Terrace	31 B3	
Glandore Road	5 B2	
Glaslyn	7 A3	
Glasnevin	3 B2	
Glasnevin Court	2 C1	
Glasnevin Downs	2 D1	
Glasnevin Hill	3 B2	
Glasnevin Ind Est	2 C2	
Glasnevin Oaks	2 D1	
Glasnevin Woods	2 C1	
Glenard Avenue	10 C2	
Glenarm Avenue	4 D3	
Glenbeigh Park	9 B2	
Glenbeigh Road	10 C2	
Glencar Road	9 B3	
Glencarthy Court	7 A2	
Glendalough Road	4 C3	
Glendinning Lane	20 C3[10]	
Glenealy Road	26 C3	
Glengarriff Crescent	12 C2	
Glengarriff Parade	12 C1	
Glenmalure Park	25 B1	
Glenmore Road	9 B2	
Gloucester Diamond	11 D3[13]	
Gloucester Lane	12 D3[8]	

Gloucester Pl Lwr	12 D3⁹	
Gloucester Pl Upr	12 D3	
Gloucester St Sth	21 A2	
Glovers Alley	20 C3	
Glovers Court	20 C3¹⁶	
Godfrey Place	10 C3	
Golden Lane	19 B3	
Goldenbridge Ave	25 A1	
Goldsmith Street	11 B2	
Gordon Place	28 C2⁵	
Gordon Street	22 C3	
Gortbeg Avenue	1 B1	
Gortbeg Drive	1 B1	
Gortbeg Park	1 B1	
Gortbeg Road	1 B1	
Gortmore Park	1 B1	
Grace Park Avenue	5 A3	
Grace Pk Gardens	5 A3	
Grace Park Heights	5 B1	
Grace Pk Meadows	6 C1	
Grace Park Road	5 B1	
Grace Park Terrace	5 B2	
Gracefield Avenue	8 D1	
Grafton Street	20 C3	
Graham's Row	11 B3⁵	
Granby Lane	11 B3	
Granby Place	20 C1	
Granby Row	11 B3	
Grand Canal Place	18 D3	
Grand Canal Quay	21 B3	
Grand Canal St Lwr	21 B3	
Grand Canal St Upr	29 B1	
Grand Canal View	25 A1	
Grand Parade	28 D2	
Grangegorman Lwr	19 A1	
Grangegorman Upr	11 A3	
Grangegorman Villas	11 A3²	
Granite Place	30 C3³	
Grant's Row	21 A3	
Grantham Place	28 C2	
Grantham Street	27 B2	
Grattan Court East	29 B1³	
Grattan Hall	29 B1⁷	
Grattan Parade	12 C1	
Grattan Place	21 B3	
Gray Square	19 A3²	
Gray Street	19 A3	
Great Western Ave	11 A2	
Great Western Sq	11 A2	
Great Western Villas	11 A2	
Greek Street	19 B2	
Green Street	19 B1	
Green Street East	22 C2	
Green Street Little	19 B1	
Greenfield Place	27 B3¹	
Greenmount Ave	27 A3	
Greenmount Court	27 A3	
Greenmount Lane	27 A3	
Greenmount Square	27 A3²	
Greenore Terrace	21 B3²	
Greenville Avenue	27 A2	
Greenville Parade	27 A2¹	
Greenville Place	27 A2⁷	
Greenville Terrace	27 A2	
Grenville Lane	12 C3	
Grenville Street	12 C3	
Griffith Avenue (Finglas)	3 A1	
Griffith Avenue (Marino)	5 B2	
Griffith Avenue (Whitehall)	4 C1	
Griffith Court	5 B3	
Griffith Downs	5 A1	
Griffith Hall	5 B2	
Griffith Lawns	4 C1	
Griffith Square	27 A2⁵	
Griffith Vale	5 B2	
Grosvenor Court	8 C3	
Grove Avenue	27 B3⁵	
Grove Park	27 B3	
Grove Road	27 B3	
Guild Street	21 B1	
Guildford Place	13 A3¹	
Haddington Place	29 B1	
Haddington Road	29 B1	
Haddington Way East	30 C1⁷	
Haddon Court	15 B2²	
Haddon Park	15 A1	
Haddon Road	15 B1	
Hagan's Court	29 A1	
Halliday Road	18 D1	
Halliday Square	18 C1	
Halpin's Row	13 A3¹¹	
Halston Street	19 B1	
Hamilton Court	19 B2⁵	
Hamilton Street	26 D1	
Hammond Lane	19 A2	
Hammond Street	27 A1	
Hampstead Park	4 C1	
Hampton Court	29 B3⁴	
Hampton Estate	8 D3	
Hampton Green	9 A1	
Hampton Square	9 B2	
Hanbury Lane	19 A3	
Hanover Court	19 B3¹⁴	
Hanover Lane	19 B3	
Hanover Quay	22 C2	
Hanover Square	19 B3	
Hanover St E	21 A2	
Hanover St W	19 A3⁹	
Harbour Court	20 D1	
Harcourt Green	28 C2¹⁵	
Harcourt Lane	28 C2¹⁰	
Harcourt Road	28 C2	
Harcourt Street	28 C1	
Harcourt Terrace	28 D2	
Hardiman Road	4 C2	
Hardwicke Arch	12 C3²	
Hardwicke Lane	12 C3³	
Hardwicke Place	12 C3⁶	
Hardwicke Street	12 C3	
Harman Street	26 D1	
Harmony Row	21 A3	
Harold Bridge Court	27 A3	
Harold Road	18 D1	
Harolds Cross	26 D3	
Harolds Cross Cotts	27 A3⁵	
Harolds Cross Rd	27 A3	
Haroldville Avenue	26 C1	
Harrington Street	27 B2	
Harry Court	27 B1⁷	
Harry Street	20 C3¹	
Harty Place	27 B1	
Hastings Street	22 C3	
Hatch Lane	28 D2	
Hatch Place	28 D2	
Hatch Street Lower	28 D2	
Hatch Street Upper	28 C2	
Hatters Lane	27 A3¹	
Havelock Square	30 C1	
Havelock Terrace	30 D1¹	
Haverty Road	14 C1	
Hawkins Street	20 D2	
Hawthorn Avenue	13 B3	
Hawthorn Terrace	13 B3	
Haymarket	19 A2	
Hazel Road	6 D1	
Hazelwood House	28 C3	
Healy Street	12 D3	
Hendrick Lane	18 D2⁵	
Hendrick Place	18 D2²	
Henrietta House	19 B1⁵	
Henrietta Lane	11 B3	
Henrietta Place	19 B1	
Henrietta Street	19 B1	
Henry Place	20 C1	
Henry Street	20 C1	
Hepenstal Terrace	31 B2¹	
Herbert Cottages	30 C2⁴	
Herbert Court	31 A3	
Herbert Lane	29 A1	
Herbert Park	30 C3	
Herbert Park Lane	30 C3	

Name	Ref
Herbert Place (Raggot Street)	29 A1
Herbert Place (Irishtown)	22 D3[4]
Herbert Road	30 D2
Herbert Street	29 A1
Herberton Drive	26 C2
Herberton Park	25 B2
Herberton Road	25 B1
Heytesbury Lane	29 B3
Heytesbury Street	27 B2
Hibernian Avenue	13 B3
High Street	19 B3
Hill Street	12 C3
Hogan Place	21 A3
Holles Place	21 A3
Holles Row	21 A3
Holles Street	21 A3
Holly Road	6 D2
Hollybank Road	4 C3
Hollybrook Court	15 A1[3]
Hollybrook Ct Dr	15 A1[2]
Hollybrook Grove	14 D1
Hollybrook Park	7 A3
Hollybrook Road	15 A1
Holycross Avenue	12 D1
Holyrood Castle	31 A3[1]
Holyrood Park	31 A3
Home Farm Park	4 D2
Home Farm Road	4 C1
Homelee	30 D2[3]
Hope Avenue	13 B2
Hope Street	22 C3
Hospital Lane	17 A2[3]
Hotel Yard	20 C1
Houghton Terrace	18 D1[1]
Howard Street	22 C3
Howth Rd (Clontarf)	7 B3
Howth Rd (Fairview)	6 D3
Howth Rd (Killester)	8 C2
Hume Street	28 D1
Huxley Crescent	26 D1[2]
Hyacinth Street	13 B3
Hybreasal	25 A1[1]
Imaal Road	10 D2
Inchicore Road	17 B3
Infirmary Road	17 B1
Ingram Road	27 A2
Innisfallen Parade	12 C2
Inns Quay	19 A2
Inver Road	9 B1
Inverness Road	13 B1
Iona Crescent	3 B3
Iona Drive	4 C3
Iona Park	3 B3
Iona Road	3 B3
Iona Villas	4 C3
Irishtown	31 A1
Irishtown Road	22 D3
Irvine Cottages	22 C1[2]
Irvine Terrace	22 C1
Irwin Court	17 B3[3]
Irwin Street	17 B3[4]
Island Street	18 D2
Island Villa	21 B3[1]
Islandbridge	17 A2
Islandbridge Court	17 A2[2]
Isolda Road	23 A3
Ivar Street	18 D1
Iveagh Buildings (Bride Rd)	19 B3[11]
Iveagh Buildings (Kevin St Upr)	27 B1[3]
Iveagh Gardens	25 A3
Ivetta Terrace	4 D3[3]
Ivy Terrace	26 D1
James Joyce Street	20 D1
James's Place E	29 A1
James's Street	18 C3
James's Street E	29 A1
James's Street N	13 B2[6]
Janeville	27 B2[7]
Jervis Lane Lower	19 B2
Jervis Lane Upper	19 B1
Jervis Street	19 B1
John Dillion Street	19 B3
John Field Road	19 B3[6]
John Street South	27 A1
John Street West	19 A3
John's Lane	19 A3
John's Lane East	19 B3
John's Street North	18 D2[4]
Johnson Court	20 C3
Johnson Place	20 C3[12]
Jones's Road	12 D2
Josephine Avenue	12 C2[10]
Joy Street	22 C3
Joyce Road	4 C2
Kearn's Place	17 A3[4]
Keeper Road	25 B2
Kelly's Lane	11 B2[6]
Kelly's Row	12 C2
Kenmare Parade	12 C1[1]
Kerlogue Road	23 A3
Kevin Barry Flats	19 A1[8]
Kevin Street Lower	27 B1
Kevin Street Upper	27 B1
Kevins Avenue	27 B1[?]
Kickham Road	25 A1
Kilalla Road	1 B3
Kilbride Road	7 B2
Kildare Place	20 D3[3]
Kildare Street	20 D3
Kilkieran Court	1 B3
Kilkieran Road	1 B3
Killan Road	22 C1
Killarney Avenue	13 A3[7]
Killarney Parade	12 C2
Killarney Street	13 A3
Killester	8 C1
Killester Avenue	7 A1/7 B2
Killester Court	7 B1
Killester Park	7 B1
Kilmainham	17 A3
Kilmainham Lane	17 B3
Kilmainham Village	18 C3[2]
Kinahan Street	18 C1
Kincora Avenue	15 B1
Kincora Drive	15 B1
Kincora Grove	15 B1
Kincora Park	16 C1
Kincora Road	16 C1
King Street North	19 A1
King Street South	20 C3
King's Avenue	13 A2[16]
Kingram Place	28 D2
Kings Court	10 D3[3]
Kings Inns Court	11 B3[13]
Kingsland Pk Ave	27 B2[3]
Kingsland Parade	27 B3
Kippure Park	1 A1
Kirkwood	31 A3
Kirwan Street	18 D1
Kirwan St Cotts	10 D3
Knightsbridge	15 B1[3]
Knocknarea Avenue	25 A3
Knocknarow Tce	17 B3[11]
Kyle-Clare Road	23 A3[1]
La Vista Avenue	7 B1
Lad Lane	29 A1
Lad Lane Upper	29 A2
Lady's Lane	17 A3
Lagan Road	1 B1
Lamb Alley	19 A3
Lambay Road	4 C1
Lambourne Village	15 B1[4]
Langan Road	2 B2
Langrishe Place	12 D3[15]
Lansdowne Cres	30 C1[4]
Lansdowne Gdns	30 C2[2]
Lansdowne Hall	30 D1[2]
Lansdowne Lane	30 C1

Lansdowne Park	30 C1	Lissadel Avenue	25 A3	Malone Gardens	30 C1
Lansdowne Road	30 C2	Lissadel Court	25 A3	Malpas Court	27 B1[4]
Lansdowne Square	30 D2	Lissadel Drive	25 A2	Malpas Street	27 A1
Lansdowne Terrace	30 C1[1]	Lissenfield	29 C3[2]	Malpas Terrace	27 B1
Lansdowne Village	30 D1	Little Britain Street	19 B1	Mander's Terrace	28 D3[3]
Lansdowne Villas	30 C1[3]	Little Mary Street	19 B2	Mannix Road	4 C3
Lawrence Grove	7 A3	Litton Lane	20 C2[1]	Manor Mews	18 D1
Le Vere Terrace	27 A3[4]	Lombard Court	21 A2[3]	Manor Place	18 D1
Lea Crescent	31 B2	Lombard Street E	21 A2	Manor Street	18 D1
Lea Road	31 B2	Lombard Street W	27 B2	Margaret Place	30 C1
Leahy's Terrace	31 A1	Lomond Avenue	5 B3	Marguerite Road	3 B3
Lee Road	2 C2	Londonbridge Drive	30 D1	Marine Drive	31 A2
Leeson Close	28 D2	Londonbridge Road	30 D1	Mariners Port	21 A1
Leeson Lane	28 D1	Long Lane	11 B3	Marino	5 B3
Leeson Park	29 A3	Long Lane Close	27 B1[9]	Marino Avenue	6 D3
Leeson Park Ave	29 A3	Long's Place	18 D3	Marino Crescent	14 C1
Leeson Place	28 D2	Longford Lane	20 C3[8]	Marino Green	6 C3
Leeson Street Lwr	28 D1	Longford St Great	19 B3[7]	Marino Mart	14 C1
Leeson Street Upr	29 A2	Longford St Little	20 C3[7]	Marino Park	6 C3
Leeson Village	29 A3	Longwood Avenue	27 B2	Marino Park Ave	14 C1
Leeson Walk	28 D3	Lord Edward Court	19 B3[12]	Marion Villas	26 D1
Leinster Avenue	13 B2	Lord Edward Street	19 B3	Mark's Alley West	19 A3
Leinster Lane	20 D3	Lord's Walk	9 A3	Mark's Lane	21 A2
Leinster Market	20 D2[6]	Loreto Road	26 D1	Market Street South	18 D3
Leinster Street E	13 B2[5]	Lorne Terrace	17 B3[14]	Marks Street	20 D2
Leinster Street N	11 A1	Lotts	20 C2	Marlborough Court	20 D1[10]
Leinster Street S	20 D3	Lourdes House	12 D3[14]	Marlborough Mews	10 C3
Leitrim Place	29 B7	Lourdes Road	26 C1	Marlborough Place	20 D1[4]
Leix Road	10 D2	Love Lane East	29 B1[2]	Marlborough Road	10 C3
Lemon Street	20 C3	Luby Road	17 A3	Marlborough Street	20 C1
Lennox Place	27 B2	Luke Street	20 D2	Marmion Court	19 A1[6]
Lennox Street	28 C2	Lullymore Terrace	26 D2	Marne Villas	11 A3
Lennox Terrace	28 C2[12]	Lurgan Street	19 B1[1]	Marrowbone Lane	18 D3
Leo Avenue	12 C2[11]	Lynch's Place	11 B2[3]	Marrowbone La Blds	18 D3[3]
Leo Street	12 C2	Lynton Court	30 D3[2]	Marrowbone La Clo	18 D3[4]
Leonard's Court	27 A2	Mabbot Lane	20 D1	Marshal Lane	18 D2
Leslie's Building	11 A2	Mabel Street	12 D1	Marshalsea Lane	18 D3[2]
Leukos Road	23 A3	Macken Street	21 B3	Martello View	31 B2
Liberty House	12 D3[11]	Macken Villa	21 B3	Martello Wood	31 B3
Liberty Lane	28 C1	Mackie's Place	28 D1	Martin Street	27 B2
Liberty Square	19 A3[12]	Mackie's Place	28 D1[3]	Martin White Chalets	30 D2[2]
Library View Tce	11 B2[1]	Madden Road	27 A1	Mary Aikenhead Ho	18 C3[4]
Liffey Street Lower	20 C2	Madison Road	25 B1	Mary's Abbey	19 B2
Liffey Street Upper	20 C1	Magdalen Terrace	22 D3[7]	Mary's Lane	19 B2
Liffey Street West	18 D2	Magenis Place	21 A2	Matt Talbot Court	12 D3[1]
Lime Street	21 A2	Magennis Square	21 A2[1]	Mauncell Place	11 B3[14]
Limekiln Lane	27 A3	Malachi Place	13 B3[1]	Maxwell Street	26 D1
Lincoln Lane	19 A2[3]	Malachi Road	18 D1	May Lane	19 A2
Lincoln Place	20 D3	Malahide Road	7 A1	May Park	7 A1
Lindsay Road	11 B1	(Donnycarney)		May Street	12 D2
Linenhall Parade	19 B1	Malahide Road	14 C1	Mayfield Road	25 B1
Linenhall Street	19 B1[4]	(Fairview)		Mayor Street Lower	21 A1
Linenhall Terrace	19 B1	Malahide Road	6 D3	Mayor Street Upper	22 C1
Lisburn Street	19 B1	(Marino)		McCarthy Terrace	26 C1[1]
Liscannor Road	1 B3	Mallin Avenue	26 C1	Mc Dowell Avenue	18 C3[1]

McKee Drive	9 B2	
McKee Park	9 B2	
McMahon Street	27 B2	
Meades Terrace	21 A3	
Meath Market	19 A3[13]	
Meath Place	19 A3	
Meath Square	19 A3[3]	
Meetinghouse Lane	19 B2[3]	
Meetinghouse Square	20 C2[13]	
Melrose Avenue	13 B1	
Memorial Road	20 D1	
Mercer Street Lwr	20 C3	
Mercer Street Upr	28 C1	
Merchamp	16 D1	
Merchant's Arch	20 C2[6]	
Merchant's Quay	19 A2	
Merchant's Road	14 D3	
Merrion Close	21 A3[2]	
Merrion Place	20 D3	
Merrion Road	30 D3	
Merrion Row	28 D1	
Merrion Sq E	29 A1	
Merrion Sq N	21 A3	
Merrion Sq S	29 A1	
Merrion Sq W	21 A3	
Merrion St Lwr	21 A3	
Merrion St Upr	28 D1	
Merry Bush	31 A2	
Merton Avenue	27 A2	
Merton Park	27 A2	
Merville Avenue	14 C1	
Mespil Estate	29 A2	
Mespil Road	29 A2	
Middle Third	8 C1	
Military Road (Kilmainham)	17 B3	
Military Road (Rathmines)	28 C3	
Mill Brook	17 B3[15]	
Mill Lane	27 A1	
Mill Street	27 A1	
Millbourne Avenue	4 C3	
Millbrook Terrace	17 A3[7]	
Millmount Avenue	4 C3	
Millmount Place	4 D3	
Millmount Terrace	4 D3	
Millmount Villas	4 C3	
Misery Hill	21 B2	
Mitchell House	29 A3[3]	
Moira Road	18 C1	
Moland Place	20 D1[2]	
Molesworth Place	20 D3[2]	
Molesworth Street	20 D3	
Molyneux Yard	19 A3	
Monck Place	11 A2	
Montague Court	28 C1[3]	
Montague Lane	28 C1	
Montague Place	28 C1	
Montague Street	28 C1	
Montpelier Drive	18 C1	
Montpelier Gardens	18 C1[2]	
Montpelier Hill	18 C1	
Montpelier Park	18 C1	
Moore Lane	20 C1	
Moore Street	20 C1	
Moracrete Cotts	25 B3[1]	
Morehampton Lane	29 B3	
Morehampton Mews	29 B3[2]	
Morehampton Sq	29 B3[1]	
Morgan Place	19 A2[4]	
Morning Star Ave	19 A1	
Morning Star Road	26 C1	
Morrogh Terrace	5 B2[1]	
Moss Street	20 D2	
Mount Brown	17 B3	
Mount Drummond Avenue	27 A3	
Mount Drummond Square	27 B3	
Mount Prospect Lwr	8 D3	
Mount St Cres	29 B1[4]	
Mount St Lower	29 B1	
Mount St Upper	29 A1	
Mount Temple Rd	18 D1	
Mountain View Ct	12 D3[18]	
Mountjoy Parade	12 D2[14]	
Mountjoy Place	12 D3	
Mountjoy Sq E	12 D3	
Mountjoy Sq N	12 D2	
Mountjoy Sq S	12 D3	
Mountjoy Sq W	12 C3	
Mountjoy Street	11 B3	
Mountjoy St Mid	11 B3[9]	
Mountpleasant Ave Lower	28 C3	
Mountpleasant Ave Upper	28 C3	
Mountpleasant Pde	28 C3[6]	
Mountpleasant Pl	28 D3[2]	
Mountpleasant Sq	28 C3	
Mountpleasant Tce	28 C3[8]	
Mountpleasant Tce Upper	28 C3[8]	
Mountpleasant Villas	28 D3[4]	
Mountshannon Rd	25 B1	
Mourne Rd	25 A2	
Moy Elta Road	13 B3	
Moyle Road	2 C2	
Muckross Parade	12 C2[2]	
Mullinahack	19 A2[9]	
Mulroy Road	2 C3	
Munster Street	11 A1	
Murtagh Road	18 D1	
Myrtle Street	11 B3	
Nassau Place	20 D3[1]	
Nassau Street	20 D3	
Navan Road	9 A1	
Nelson Street	11 B2	
Nephin Road	9 A1	
Nerney's Court	12 C3	
New Bride Street	27 B1	
New Grove Avenue	31 B2	
New Ireland Road	25 B1	
New Row South	27 A1	
New Row Square	27 A1	
New Street Grdns	27 B1[8]	
New Street North	19 A1	
New Street South	27 B1	
New Wapping St	22 C1	
Newbridge Avenue	30 D1	
Newbridge Drive	30 D1	
Newcomen Avenue	13 A2	
Newcomen Court	13 A2[7]	
Newgrange Road	10 D1	
Newmarket	27 A1	
Newmarket Street	27 A1	
Newport Street	18 D3	
Niall Street	10 C3	
Nicholas Avenue	19 A1	
Nicholas Street	19 B3	
Nore Road	2 C2	
Norfolk Road	11 A1	
Norseman Court	18 D1	
Norseman Place	18 D1	
North Circular Road	10 C3	
North Circular Road	12 D2	
North Quay Ext	22 D2	
North Road	9 A2	
North Strand Road	13 A3	
North Wall	21 B1	
North Wall Quay	21 B2	
Northbrook Avenue	28 D3	
Northbrook Ave Lwr	13 B2	
Northbrook Ave Upr	13 B2	
Northbrook Lane	28 D3	
Northbrook Road	28 D3	
Northbrook Terrace	13 B2[7]	
Northland Drive	2 D1	
Northland Grove	2 D1	
Northumberland Rd	29 B1	
Northumberland Sq	20 D1[5]	
Norton's Avenue	11 A2	
Nottingham Street	13 B2	
O'Briens Place N	4 C2	

Name	Grid
O'Briens Terrace	11 B1
O'Carolan Road	27 A1
O'Connell Avenue	11 B2
O'Connell Gardens	30 D1
O'Connell St Upr	20 C1
O'Connell St Lwr	20 C1
O'Curry Avenue	27 A1⁵
O'Curry Road	27 A1
O'Daly Road	4 C2
O'Devaney Gardens	18 C1
O'Donovan Road	27 A2
O'Hara Avenue	27 B3
O'Leary Road	25 A1
O'Neachtain Road	4 C2¹
O'Neill's Buildings	28 C1⁴
O'Quinn Avenue	18 C3
O'Rahilly House	22 D3¹¹
O'Rahilly Parade	20 C1
O'Reilly Avenue	17 B3
O'Sullivan Avenue	13 A2
Oak Road	6 D2
Oakfield Place	27 B2
Oaklands Drive	31 A2
Oaklands Park	30 D2
Oakley Park	8 D3
Observatory Lane	28 C3¹
Offaly Road	10 D1
Olaf Road	18 D1
Old Cabra Road	10 C2
Old County Glen	25 B3
Old County Road	25 B3
Old Kilmainham	17 B3
Old Mill Court	27 B1¹
Old Mountpleasant	28 D3
Oliver Plunkett Ave	22 D3
Oliver Bond House	19 A2⁶
Oliver Bond Street	19 A2
Ontario Terrace	28 C3
Orchard Lane	28 D3
Orchard Road	13 A1
Orchard View	11 A3¹
Oriel Hall	21 A1
Oriel Place	13 B3
Oriel Street Lower	13 B3
Oriel Street Upper	21 A1
Ormeau Street	22 C3¹
Ormond Place	19 B2⁴
Ormond Quay Lwr	20 C2
Ormond Quay Upr	19 B2
Ormond Road	4 D3
Ormond Square	19 B2
Ormond Street	27 A1
Osbourne Terrace	28 D3⁸
Oscar Square	27 A1
Ossory Road	13 B3
Ostman Place	18 D1
Oswald Road	31 A1
Oulton Park	16 C1
Our Lady's Close	26 D1⁵
Our Lady's Road	26 D1
Ovoca Road	27 B2
Owens Avenue	17 B3⁷
Oxford Road	28 D3
Oxmantown Lane	19 A2
Oxmantown Road	10 C3
Palace Street	20 C2¹²
Palatine Square	18 C1
Palmerston Place	11 B3
Paradise Place	11 B3
Park Avenue	31 A3
Park Avenue West	18 C2²
Park Court	31 A3
Park Lane	31 A3
Park Lane East	20 D2
Park Mews	29 B3
Park Place	17 A2¹
Park Springs	9 A1
Park Terrace	19 A3¹⁰
Park View	9 B2
Parkgate Street	18 C2
Parkview Court	9 A2¹
Parkview Place	22 D3³
Parliament Row	20 C2¹⁰
Parliament Street	19 B2
Parnell Avenue	27 A3
Parnell Court	27 A3
Parnell Place	12 C3
Parnell Road	26 D2
Parnell Sq East	12 C3
Parnell Sq North	12 C3
Parnell Sq West	12 C3
Parnell Street	12 C3/20 C1
Patrick Street	19 B3
Pearse Grove	21 B3⁴
Pearse House	21 A2
Pearse Square	21 B2
Pearse Street	20 D2
Pembroke Cottages	22 D2
Pembroke Gardens	29 B2
Pembroke Lane	29 A1
Pembroke Park	29 B3
Pembroke Place	28 D2²
Pembroke Place (Ballsbridge)	30 C3²
Pembroke Road	29 B2
Pembroke Road	30 C1
Pembroke Row	29 A1
Pembroke Square	21 B3
Pembroke Street	22 D3
Pembroke St Lwr	28 D1
Pembroke St Upr	28 D1
Penrose Street	22 C3
Percy Lane	29 B1
Percy Place	29 B1
Peter Place	28 C2
Peter Row	28 C1
Peter Street	19 B3
Peterson's Court	21 A2²
Petrie Road	27 A2
Phibsboro	11 A2
Phibsboro	11 B2
Phibsborough Ave	11 A2
Phibsborough Place	11 B2⁵
Phibsborough Road	11 B2
Philipsburgh Ave	5 B3/13 B1
Philipsburgh Terrace	5 B3
Philomena Terrace	22 D3⁵
Phoenix Court	18 C1
Phoenix Manor	10 C3
Phoenix Street N	19 A2
Pig Lane	12 D3
Pigeon House Road	24 C3
Pigeon House Rd (Ringsend)	23 A2
Pim Street	18 D3
Pimlico	19 A3
Pimlico Cottages	19 A3¹⁸
Pine Hurst	9 B1
Pine Road	23 A3
Pleasants Lane	28 C1
Pleasants Place	28 C1
Pleasants Street	27 B1
Polo Road	9 A3
Poolbeg Quay	23 A3
Poolbeg Street	20 D2
Poole Street	19 A3¹⁹
Poplar Row	13 B2
Poplar Row (Apts)	13 B2⁴
Port Tunnell	14 D3
Port View House	22 D2
Portland Close	13 A3⁵
Portland Court	12 D2³
Portland Place	12 C2
Portland Row	13 A3
Portland Square	12 D2⁸
Portland Street N	12 D2
Portland Street W	18 D3
Portmahon Drive	25 B1
Portobello Harbour	28 C2
Portobello Place	28 C2¹³
Portobello Road	27 B3
Portside Business C.	14 C2
Portside Court	14 C2
Power's Court	29 B1
Power's Square	19 B3¹⁵

Prebend Street 19 A1
Preston Street 13 A3[8]
Price's Lane 20 C2
(Aston Quay)
Price's Lane 28 C3
(Ranelagh)
Priestfield Cottages 26 D2[1]
Priestfield Drive 26 D2[2]
Primrose Avenue 11 B3
Primrose Street 11 B3[3]
Prince of Wales Tce 30 D3[1]
Prince's St Sth 21 A2
Prince's St Nth 20 C1
Prior Hall 18 C3[3]
Proby's Lane 20 C1
Promenade Road 15 A3
Prospect Avenue 3 B3
Prospect Road 11 B1
Prospect Square 3 B3
Prospect Terrace 17 A3[6]
(Kilmainham)
Prospect Terrace 31 A1[4]
(Sandymount)
Prospect Way 3 B3
Protestant Row 28 C1[2]
Proud's Lane 28 C1
Prussia Street 10 D3
Pyro Villas 26 D1
Quarry Cottages 7 B2[1]
Quarry Road 10 C1
Quartiere Bloom 20 C2
Queen Street 19 A2
Quinn's Lane 28 D1
Raglan Lane 29 B2
Raglan Road 29 B2
Railway Cottages 30 D2[1]
Railway Street 12 D3
Railway Terrace 21 B3
Rainsford Avenue 18 D3[1]
Rainsford Street 18 D3
Raleigh Square 25 A3
Ranelagh 28 D3
Ranelagh Avenue 28 D3
Rath Row 20 D2[2]
Rathdown Road 11 A2
Rathdown Square 10 D3
Rathdrum Road 26 C3
Rathlin Road 4 C1
Rathmines 27 C3
Rathmines Rd Lwr 28 C3
Ratoath Estate 1 A2
Ratoath Road 1 A2
Ravensdale Road 14 C3
Raymond Street 27 A2
Red Cow Lane 19 A1

Redmond's Hill 28 C1
Reginald Square 19 A3[4]
Reginald Street 19 A3
Rehoboth Avenue 26 D2
Rehoboth Place 26 C2
Reilly's Avenue 26 C2
Reuben Avenue 26 C1
Reuben Street 26 C1
Rialto Buildings 26 C1
Rialto Cottages 25 B1
Rialto Drive 25 B2
Rialto Place 26 C1[4]
Rialto Street 26 C1
Richmond Avenue 13 A1
Richmond Cottages 13 A2[3]
Richmond Cotts N 13 A2
Richmond Crescent 13 A2[2]
Richmond Estate 13 B1
Richmond Hill 28 C3
Richmond Lane 12 D2[12]
Richmond Mews 28 C3
Richmond Parade 13 A2[10]
Richmond Place 28 C3
Richmond Pl Sth 28 C2[9]
Richmond Road 4 D3/13 A1
Richmond Row 28 C2
Richmond St Nth 13 A2
Richmond St Sth 28 C2
Richmond Villas 28 C2[4]
Ringsend 22 D3
Ringsend Park 22 D2
Ringsend Road 22 C3
River Gardens 3 B2
Riverbank Hall 3 A1
Riverston Abbey 1 A2
Robert Emmett Close 18 D3
Robert Place 12 D1[1]
Robert Street 18 D3
Robert Street 12 D1
(Drumcondra)
Robert Street South 18 D3
Roe Lane 18 D2
Roger's Lane 28 D1
Roosevelt Cottages 9 A1
Rope Walk Place 22 D3
Rosary Road 26 C1
Rosary Terrace 22 D3
Rosedale Terrace 27 B2[2]
Rosemount 7 A1
Rosemount Court 17 A3[1]
Rosemount Road 11 A2
Rosemount Terrace 18 C3
Rosevale Court 8 D1
Rosevale Mansions 8 D1
Ross Road 19 B3

Ross Street 10 C3
Rostrevor Terrace 21 B3[3]
Rothe Abbey 25 A1
Rowerstown Lane 17 A3[3]
Royal Canal Bank 11 B2
Royal Canal Court 11 B2[13]
Royal Canal Tce 11 A3
Royse Road 11 B1
Russell Avenue 12 D2
Russell Ave East 13 B3
Russell Street 12 D2
Rutland Avenue 26 C3
Rutland Cottages 12 D3[4]
Rutland Court 12 D3
Rutland Place North 12 D3
Rutland Place West 12 C3
Rutland St Lower 12 D3
Rutledge Terrace 26 D2
Ryder's Row 19 B1
Sackville Avenue 13 A2
Sackville Gardens 13 A2[1]
Sackville Place 20 C1
St Agatha Court 13 A3[10]
St Aidan's Park 6 C3
St Aidan's Pk Ave 6 C3
St Aidan's Pk Rd 14 C1
St Alban's Street 27 A2
St Alphonsus Avenue 12 C1[1]
St Alphonsus Rd Lwr 12 C1
St Alphonsus Rd Upr 12 C1
St Andrews Lane 20 C3[11]
St Andrews Street 20 C3
St Anne's (apts.) 28 D3
St Anne's Rd Nth 12 C1
St Anne's Rd Sth 26 D2
St Anne's Terrace 28 D3
St Anthony's Place 12 C3[1]
St Anthony's Road 26 C1
St Attracta Road 2 C3
St Audoen's House 19 A2[5]
St Audoen's Tce 19 B3[4]
St Augustine Street 19 A2
St Barnaba's Gdns 13 B3
St Benedict's Gdns 13 C2[4]
St Brendan's Cotts 22 D3
St Brendan's Road 12 C1
St Bricin's Park 18 C1
St Brigid's Avenue 13 B2
St Brigid's Cotts 13 B2[9]
St Brigid's Court 7 B1
St Brigid's Drive 7 B1
St Brigid's Road 8 C1
St Brigid's Rd Upr 12 C1
St Catherine's Ave 26 D2
St Catherine's La W 19 A3

St Clare's Avenue 27 A3
St Clement's Road 12 C1²
St Columba's Rd Lwr 12 C1
St Columba's Rd Upr 12 C1
St David's Court 15 B1⁵
St David's Terrace 10 C3
(Blackhorse Ave)
St David's Terrace 3 B1
(Glasnevin)
St David's Wood 7 A1
St Declan's Road 6 C3
St Declan's Terrace 6 C3
St Eithne Road 10 D1
St Elizabeth's Ct 10 D2
St Finbar's Road 2 C3
St Finbarr's Court 1 B3¹
St Fintan Road 10 D1
St Fintan Terrace 2 D3
St Francis Square 19 B3¹
St George's Ave 12 D1
St Helena's Road 1 B1
St Ignatius Avenue 12 C2
St Ignatius Road 12 C1
St Ita's Road 3 B2¹
St James Place 31 A2⁴
St James's Avenue 13 A2
St James's Avenue 18 C3
St James's Terrace 26 C2
(Dolphin's Barn)
St James's Terrace 31 A1¹
(Sandymount)
St James's Walk 26 C1
St Jarlath Road 10 D1
St John's Avenue 19 A3⁵
St John's Cottages 17 B3²
St John's Court 6 D2¹
St John's Court 7 A2
St John's Rd West 17 B2
St John's Street 27 A1¹
St John's Terrace 17 B3¹²
St John's Wood 15 B1²
St Joseph's Avenue 13 A1
(Clonliffe Road)
St Joseph's Avenue 12 C1
(Drumcondra)
St Joseph's Cotts 13 A3¹³
St Joseph's Court 10 D3²
St Joseph's Mansions 13 A3
St Joseph's Parade 11 B2
St Joseph's Place 11 B3⁸
(Phibsborough)
St Joseph's Place 10 D3
(Prussia Street)
St Joseph's Road 10 D3
St Joseph's Square 16 D2²

St Joseph's Street 12 C2⁷
St Joseph's Terrace 12 D2¹³
(North Circular Rd)
St Joseph's Tce 13 B1³
(Marino)
St Joseph's Tce 22 D3¹²
(Ringsend)
St Joseph's Villas 13 A2⁹
St Kevin's Cotts 27 B2¹
St Kevin's Parade 27 B2
St Kevin's Road 27 B3
St Laurence Place 11 B3²
St Laurence Pl E 21 B1¹
St Lawrence Road 15 A1
St Lawrence's Court 7 A3
St Luke's Avenue 27 A1
St Luke's Gate 27 A1
St Maignenn's Tce 17 B3⁶
St Malachy Road 4 C2
St Margaret's Ave 19 A3⁶
(Pimlico)
St Margaret's Ave 26 D1¹
(Cork Street)
St Margaret's Ave N 12 D2¹¹
St Margarets Tce 26 D1
St Mary's Ave Nth 11 B3⁶
St Mary's Lane 29 B1⁵
St Mary's Mansions 12 D3¹⁰
St Mary's Place Nth 11 B3
St Mary's Rd Nth 14 C3
St Mary's Rd Sth 29 B2
St Mary's Terrace 18 D1³
(Arbour Hill)
St Mary's Terrace 11 B3
(Phibsborough)
St Mary's Terrace 22 D3¹⁴
(Ringsend)
St Michael's Close 19 B3¹⁰
St Michael's Hill 19 B3⁸
St Michael's Place 11 B3¹⁵
St Michael's Road 4 C2
St Michael's Tce 27 A1
St Michan's House 19 B2⁶
St Michan's Lane 19 B2⁷
St Michan's Street 19 B2
St Mobhi Boithrin 3 B1
St Mobhi Court 3 B1
St Mobhi Drive 3 B2
St Mobhi Grove 3 B2
St Mobhi Road 3 B2
St Mura's Terrace 13 B3²
St Nicholas Place 19 B3
St Patrick's Avenue 13 B2³
St Patrick's Close 27 B1
St Patrick's Parade 12 C1

St Patrick's Place 11 B3¹
St Patrick's Road 12 C1
St Patrick's Terrace 12 D1²
(Fitzroy Ave)
St Patrick's Terrace 12 D2⁹
(Russell St)
St Patrick's Villas 22 D3
St Paul Street 19 A1
St Peter's Avenue 11 A2
St Peter's Court 11 B2²
St Peter's Road 11 A2
St Philomena's Rd 3 A3
St Stephen's Gn E 28 D1
St Stephen's Gn N 20 D3
St Stephen's Gn S 28 C1
St Stephen's Gn W 28 C1
St Teresa Place 3 B3
St Teresa Road 3 B3
St Teresa's Gdns 26 D2
St Thomas Road 27 A1
St Ultan's Flats 28 C2⁸
St Vincent's Court 6 C1¹
St Vincent St Nth 11 B2⁸
St Vincent St Sth 27 B2
Saddlers Court 28 C3
Sampson's Lane 20 C1
Sandford Avenue 26 D2
Sandford Gardens 27 A2
Sandford Park 27 A2²
Sandwith St Lwr 21 A2
Sandwith St Upr 21 A3
Sandymount 31 A2
Sandymount Ave 30 D3
Sandymount Castle 31 A2³
Sandymount Cas Dr 31 A2
Sandymount Cas Pk 31 B2
Sandymount Cas Rd 31 A2
Sandymount Court 31 A1²
Sandymount Green 31 A2²
Sandymount Road 31 A1
Sarah Place 17 A2
Sarsfield Street 11 B2⁹
Sarsfield Quay 18 D2
School Street 18 D3
Schoolhouse Lane 20 D3
Schoolhouse La W 19 B3³
Seafield Avenue 16 D1
Seafield Court 16 C1¹
Seafield Road East 16 D1
Seafield Road West 16 C1
Seafort Avenue 31 A2
Seafort Cottages 31 A2
Seafort Gardens 31 A1
Seafort Terrace 31 A2¹
Seafort Villas 31 A2

Sean MacDermott St Lower 12 D3
Sean MacDermott St Upper 12 D2
Sean Moore Road 23 A3
Sean O'Casey Ave 12 D3
Seapoint Terrace 22 D3[15]
Seaview Ave E 14 C3
Seaview Ave Nth 15 A1
Second Avenue 21 B1
Selskar Terrace 28 D3
Serpentine Avenue 30 D3
Serpentine Park 30 D2
Serpentine Road 30 D2
Serpentine Terrace 30 D2
Seven Oaks 5 A1
Seville Place 12 B1/13 A3
Seville Terrace 13 A3
Shamrock Cottages 13 A3[3]
Shamrock Place 13 A3[2]
Shamrock Street 11 B3
Shamrock Terrace 13 A3
Shandon Crescent 10 D1
Shandon Drive 11 A1
Shandon Gardens 2 D3
Shandon Park 11 A1
Shandon Road 11 A1
Shanganagh Road 4 C3
Shannon Terrace 17 B3[5]
Shaw Street 20 D2
Shaw's Lane 30 C1
Shea's Court 10 D3[5]
Shelbourne Avenue 30 C2
Shelbourne Lane 30 C2[1]
Shelbourne Road 30 C1
Shellysbanks Road 24 C3
Shelmalier Road 14 C3
Shelmartin Avenue 5 B3
Shelmartin Terrace 5 B3
Sheriff Street Lower 21 A1
Sheriff Street Upper 21 B1
Sherkin Gardens 4 D1
Sherrard Avenue 12 C2
Sherrard Court 12 C2[6]
Sherrard St Lwr 12 D2
Sherrard St Upr 12 C2
Ship Street Great 19 B3
Ship Street Little 19 B3
Shrewsbury 31 A3
Sibthorpe Lane 29 A3
Sigurd Road 18 D1
Simmon's Place 12 D3[2]
Simmonscourt Road 30 D3
Simpson's Lane 22 D3[16]
Sion Hill Court 5 B1

Sion Hill Road 5 B1
Sir John Rogerson's Quay 21 B2
Sitric Place 18 D1[1]
Sitric Road 18 D1
Skreen Road 9 A1
Slade Row 18 C1
Slane Road 25 B3
Slaney Close 2 C2
Slaney Road 2 C2
Slemish Road 9 A2
Slievenamon Road 25 A1
Smithfield 19 A2
Smithfield Terrace 19 A1[5]
Somerset Street 22 C3
South Bank Road 23 B3
South Circular Rd (Dolphin's Barn) 26 C2
South Circular Rd (Islandbridge) 17 A2
South Circular Rd (Kilmainham) 25 B1
South Dock Place 22 C3
South Dock Road 22 C3
South Dock Street 22 C3
South Link Road 31 A1
South Lotts Road 22 C3
Spa Road 9 A3
Spafield Terrace 30 D3[3]
Spencer Dock 21 B1
Spencer Place 13 B2[11]
Spencer Row 20 D1[3]
Spencer St North 13 B2
Spencer St South 27 B2
Spencer Terrace 26 D1[3]
Spitalfields 19 A3[11]
Spring Avenue 13 A2
Spring Garden La 20 D2
Spring Garden St 13 A2
Springfield 9 A2
Stable Lane (Leeson Street) 28 D1
Stable Lane (Arran Qy) 19 A2
Stable Lane (Harcourt St) 28 C1
Stamer Street 27 B2
Stanhope Street 19 A1[2]
Stanley Street 19 A1
Steeven's Lane 18 C2
Stella Avenue 4 C1
Stella Gardens 22 D3
Stephen Street Lower 20 C3

Stephen Street Upper 19 B3
Stephen's Lane 29 A1
Stephens Place 29 A1
Stephens Road 25 A1
Stirrup Lane 19 A1
Stoke's Place 28 C1
Stoney Road 13 B2
Stoneybatter 18 D1
Store Street 20 D1
Strand Road 31 B2
Strand Street 23 A3
Strand Street Great 19 B2
Strand Street Little 19 B2
Strandville Avenue 13 B2
Strandville Ave E 15 A1[4]
Strandville Ave E 14 D1
Strandville House 15 A1[1]
Strandville Place 13 B2[6]
Strangford Gardens 13 B3
Strangford Rd East 13 B3
Strasburg Terrace 22 D3[8]
Strongs Court 20 C1[2]
Suffolk Street 20 C2
Suir Road 25 A1
Sullivan Street 17 B1[1]
Summer Arch 12 D2
Summer Place 12 D3
Summer St North 12 D3
Summer St South 18 D3
Summerhill 12 D3
Summerhill Parade 13 A2
Summerhill Place 12 D3
Summerville 16 C2
Sundrive Road 25 B3
Susan Terrace 27 A1
Susanville Road 13 A1
Sussex Road 29 A2
Sussex Terrace 28 D2[3]
Swan Alley 19 A3
Swan Grove 29 A3
Swan Place 29 A3
Swanard Court 26 D3
Sweeney's Terrace 27 A1
Swift's Alley 19 A3
Swift's Row 20 C2
Swilly Road 9 B1
Sword Street 18 C1
Swords Road 5 A1
Sybil Hill Road 8 D2
Sycamore Street 20 C2
Sydenham Road 30 D3
Synge Lane 27 B2
Synge Place 28 C2
Synge Street 28 C2

Synnott Place	12 C2	Thorncastle Street	22 D2	Vernon Park	8 D3
Synnott Row	12 C2[8]	Thorndale Drive	7 A1	Vernon Rise	8 D2
Taaffe's Place	13 B2	Thorndale Grove	7 A1	Vernon Street	27 B1
Talbot Lane	20 D1[7]	Thundercut Alley	19 A1	Veronica Terrace	22 D3[6]
Talbot Place	20 D1	Tolka Cottages	2 D1	Verschoyle Court	29 B1
Talbot Street	20 D1	Tolka Estate Road	2 D1	Verschoyle Place	29 A1
Tangier Lane	20 C3[15]	Tolka Quay Road	23 A1	Vicar Street	19 A3
Tara Street	20 D2	Tolka Road	13 A1	Victoria Cottages	22 D3[13]
Taylor's Lane	18 D3	Tolka Vale	2 C1	Victoria Lane	4 D3
Temple Bar	20 C2	Tolka Valley Road	1 A1	Victoria Quay	18 D2
Temple Bar Square	20 C2[15]	Tom Clarke House	13 A1[1]	Victoria Road	15 B1
Temple Buildings	11 B3[10]	Tom Kelly Road	28 C2	Victoria Street	27 B2
Temple Cottages	11 B3	Tomar Court	18 C1[4]	Victoria Villas	6 D3
Temple Court	18 C1	Torlogh Gardens	13 B1	Viking Harbour	18 D2[3]
Temple Lane North	12 C3	Torlogh Parade	5 B2[2]	Viking Place	18 D1
Temple Lane South	20 C2	Tower View Cotts	3 A3	Viking Road	18 D1
Temple Place	28 D3	Townsend Street	20 D2	Violet Hill Drive	2 D1
Temple Street West	18 C2	Traynor Place	17 B3[13]	Violet Hill Park	2 D1
Temple Villas	18 C1[3]	Trinity Square	21 A2[4]	Violet Hill Road	2 D1
Terminal Rd Nth	24 D1	Trinity Street	20 C2	Walker's Cottages	28 C3
Terminal Rd Sth	24 D1	Trinity Terrace	13 A2[13]	Walker's Court	28 C3[7]
Terrace Place	12 D3[5]	Tritonville Avenue	31 A1	Walnut Avenue	4 D1
The Anchorage	22 C3[3]	Tritonville Close	31 A1[3]	Walnut Lawn	4 D1
The Appian Way	29 A3	Tritonville Court	31 A2	Walnut Park	4 D1
The Bramblings	7 B2	Tritonville Crescent	31 A1	Walnut Rise	4 D1
The Cloisters	5 A1	Tritonville Mews	31 A1[5]	Walsh Road	4 C2
The Copse	5 A2	Tritonville Road	30 D1	Walworth Street	27 B2[5]
The Court	15 A1	Turvey Avenue	17 A3[2]	Ward's Hill	27 A1
The Crescent	5 A1	Tyrrel's Lane	22 D3[9]	Warner's Lane	28 D2
The Granary	18 D3	Tyrrell Place	12 D2[15]	Warren Street	27 B2
The Grove	5 A1	Ulster Street	11 A1	Warrenmount	27 A1[9]
The Haven	3 B1	Ulster Terrace	13 A2[5]	Warrenmount Place	27 A1[2]
The Meadows	8 D1	Upper Cross Road	25 B1	Warrenpoint	15 B1[1]
The Mews	7 B1	Usher Street	19 A2	Warrington Lane	29 B1
The Mews	15 B1	Usher's Island	18 D2	Warrington Place	29 B1
The Orchard	8 C1	Usher's Lane	19 A2[8]	Warwick Terrace	29 A3[1]
The Paddocks	25 A1	Usher's Quay	19 A2	Washington Street	27 A2
(South Circular Rd)		Valentia Parade	12 C2	Waterfall Avenue	5 A3
The Paddocks	15 B1	Valentia Road	4 C1	Waterloo Avenue	13 B2
The Pines	8 C1	Vauxhall Avenue	26 C1	Waterloo Lane	29 A3
The Square	22 D3	Vavasour Square	30 C1	Waterloo Road	29 A3
The Square	30 C1[8]	Venetian Hall	8 C1	Waterside Flats	22 C3[2]
The Stiles Road	7 B3	Ventry Drive	1 A3	Watkin's Buildings	27 A1[6]
The Sweepstakes	30 C2[7]	Ventry Park	1 A3	Watling Street	18 D2
The Turrets	30 D2	Ventry Road	1 B3	Waverley Avenue	13 B1
The Village	4 D1	Vera Terrace	4 C2[2]	Weaver Lane	11 B2[4]
The Willows	2 D2	Vernon Avenue	8 C2/16 D1	Weaver's Close	27 A1[7]
Third Avenue	21 B1	Vernon Court	16 D2	Weaver's Street	27 A1
Thomas Court	18 D3	(Clontarf Road)		Weaver's Square	27 A1[10]
Thomas Davis St Sth	19 A3	Vernon Court	16 D1	Wellesley Place	12 D2[10]
Thomas Lane	20 C1	(Seafield Road)		Wellington Lane	29 B3
Thomas St West	18 D3	Vernon Drive	8 D2	Wellington Place	29 B3
Thompson's Cotts	12 D3[3]	Vernon Gardens	16 D1	Wellington Pl Nth	11 B3[4]
Thor Place	18 C1[1]	Vernon Grove	16 D1	Wellington Quay	20 C2
Thorncastle Court	22 D2	Vernon Heath	8 D3	Wellington Road	29 B2

Street	Page	Grid Ref.
Wellington Road (Phoenix Park)	17	A2
Wellington St Lwr	11	B3
Wellington St Upr	11	B3
Wellpark Avenue	4	D1
Werburgh Street	19	B3
Wesley Place	27	A2
West Road	13	B3
Western Road	26	D2
Western Way	11	B3
Westland Row	21	A3
Westland Square	21	A2⁶
Westmoreland St	20	C2
Wexford Street	28	C1
Whelan House	22	D3¹⁰
Whitebank Road	23	B3
Whitefriar Gardens	19	B3¹³
Whitefriar Place	20	C3⁹
Whitefriar Street	19	B3
Whitehall	5	A1
Whites Lane North	11	B3¹¹
Whitworth Avenue	12	D2²
Whitworth Parade	12	C1⁴
Whitworth Place	12	C1³
Whitworth Road	11	B1
Whitworth Terrace	12	D1³
Wicklow Street	20	C3
Widow's Houses	19	A3²⁰
Wigan Road	11	B1
Wilfield	31	A3
Wilfield Park	31	A3
Wilfield Road	31	A3
Willbrook House	28	D3⁶
William St Nth	13	A2
William St Sth	20	C3
William's Lane	20	C1
William's Pl Lwr	12	D2⁴
William's Place Sth	27	B1
William's Pl Upr	12	C2⁵
Willie Bermingham Pl	17	B3¹
Willowfield	31	B3
Wilson Terrace	19	A3
Wilson's Terrace	21	A3¹
Wilton Court	29	A2¹
Wilton Place	29	A2
Wilton Terrace	29	A2
Windele Road	4	C2
Windmill Lane	21	A2
Windmill Road	25	A3
Windsor Avenue	13	B1
Windsor Place	28	D1
Windsor Terrace	27	B3
Windsor Villas	13	B1²
Winetavern Street	19	B2
Winton Road	29	A3
Wolfe Tone Quay	18	C2
Wolfe Tone Street	19	B1
Wolseley Street	27	A2³
Wood Lane	18	D2¹
Wood Quay	19	B2
Wood Street	19	B3
Woodville Road	4	C3¹
Wormwood Gate	19	A2⁷
Xavier Road	13	B2
Yarnhall Street	19	B1²
York Road	22	D2
York Street	28	C1
Zardoz Court	30	C3⁴
Zoo Road	17	A1

LIST OF STREETS
NOT NAMED ON MAP
AND SHOWN BY
SMALL NUMBERS

Page	Grid Ref.		Street Name
1	A2	1	Cloister Court
1	B3	1	St Finbarr's Court
2	D1	1	Bellevue Cottages
2	D3	1	Coke Ovens Cotts
3	B2	1	St Ita's Road
4	C2	1	O'Neachtain Road
		2	Vera Terrace
4	C3	1	Woodville Road
4	D2	1	Beaucourt
4	D3	1	Edgewood
		2	Clonturk Gardens
		3	Ivetta Terrace
5	B2	1	Morrogh Road
		2	Torlogh Parade
6	C2	1	St Vincent's Court
6	D2	1	St John's Court
		2	Cherrymount Grove
		3	Cherrymount Cres
7	B2	1	Quarry Cottages
8	D3	1	Duncan Court
9	A2	1	Parkview Court
10	C3	1	Ashford Place
		2	Ashford Cottages
10	D1	1	Fertullagh Road
10	D3	1	Aughrim Villas
		2	St Joseph's Court
		3	Kings Court
		4	Aughrim Court
		5	Shea's Court
11	A1	1	Connaught Parade
11	A2	1	Castle Terrace
11	A3	1	Orchard View
		2	Grangegorman Villas
11	B2	1	Library View Tce
		2	St Peter's Court
		3	Lynch's Place
		4	Weaver Lane
		5	Kelly's Lane
		6	Phibsborough Place
		7	Aranmore Avenue
		8	St Vincent St Nth
		9	Sarsfield Street
		10	Bective Square
		11	Royal Canal Court
		12	George's Wharf
		13	Blessington Place
11	B3	1	St Patrick's Place
		2	St Laurence Place
		3	Primrose Street
		4	Wellington Pl Nth
		5	Graham's Row
		6	St Mary's Ave Nth
		7	Blessington Court
		8	St Joseph's Place
		9	Mountjoy St Middle
		10	Temple Buildings
		11	White's Lane North
		12	Broadstone Avenue
		13	Kings Inn Court
		14	Mauncell Place
		15	St Michael's Place
		16	Delvin Terrace
12	C1	1	St Alphonsus Ave
		2	St Clement's Road
		3	Whitworth Place
		4	Whitworth Parade
12	C2	1	Kenmare Parade
		2	Muckross Parade
		3	Derrynane Parade
		4	St Benedict's Gdns
		5	Williams Place Upr
		6	Sherrard Court
		7	St Joseph's Street
		8	Synnott Row
		9	De Valera Place
		10	Josephine Avenue
		11	Leo Avenue
		12	George's Place
12	C3	1	St Anthony's Place
		2	Hardwicke Arch
		3	Hardwicke Lane
		4	Frederick Court
		5	Gardiner Row
		6	Hardwicke Place
		7	Frederick Lane Nth

	8 Bethesda Place	11 Foster Place North
	9 Cavendish Row	12 Ballybough Lane
	10 Britain Place	13 Trinity Terrace
12 D1	1 Robert Place	14 Ballybough Court
	2 St Patrick's Terrace	15 Ballybough Avenue
	(Fitzroy Ave)	16 King's Avenue
	3 Whitworth Terrace	17 Catherine Court
12 D2	1 Drumcondra Park	13 A3 1 Guildford Place
	2 Whitworth Avenue	2 Shamrock Place
	3 Portland Court	3 Shamrock Cottages
	4 William's Place Lwr	4 Duke Row
	5 Belvidere Avenue	5 Portland Close
	6 Campbell's Lane	6 Buckingham Place
	7 Campbell's Row	7 Killarney Avenue
	8 Portland Square	8 Preston Street
	9 St Patrick's Tce	9 Beaver Close
	(Russell St)	10 St Agatha Court
	10 Wellesley Place	11 Halpin's Row
	11 St Margaret's Ave Nth	12 Aldborough Square
	12 Richmond Lane	13 St Joseph's Cotts
	13 St Joseph's Tce	13 B1 1 Caragh Court
	(N.C.Rd)	2 Windsor Villas
	14 Mountjoy Parade	3 St Joseph's Tce
	15 Tyrrell's Place	(Marino)
	16 Brendan Behan Ct	13 B2 1 Courtney Place
12 D3	1 Matt Talbot Court	2 Annesley Avenue
	2 Simmon's Place	3 St Patrick's Avenue
	3 Thompson's Cotts	4 Poplar Row (Apt)
	4 Rutland Cottages	5 Leinster Street East
	5 Terrace Place	6 James's Street Nth
	6 Bella Place	7 Northbrook Terrace
	7 Bella Avenue	8 Strandville Place
	8 Gloucester Lane	9 St Brigid's Cotts
	9 Gloucester Pl Lwr	10 Austin's Cottages
	10 St Mary's Mansions	11 Spencer Place
	11 Liberty House	13 B3 1 Malachi Place
	12 Buckingham Village	2 St Mura's Terrace
	13 Gloucester Diamond	14 C3 1 Boolavogue Road
	14 Lourdes House	14 D1 1 Crescent House
	15 Langrishe Place	15 A1 1 Strandville House
	16 Belmont Place	2 Hollybrook Ct Drive
	17 Father Scully House	3 Hollybrook Court
	18 Mountain View Ct	4 Strandville Ave East
	19 Avondale House	15 B1 1 Warrenpoint
13 A1	1 Tom Clarke House	2 St John's Wood
13 A2	1 Sackville Gardens	3 Knightsbridge
	2 Richmond Crescent	4 Lambourne Village
	3 Richmond Cottages	5 St David's Court
	4 Clonmore Villas	15 B2 1 Alverno
	5 Ulster Terrace	2 Haddon Court
	6 Clinch's Court	16 C1 1 Seafield Court
	7 Newcomen Court	16 D2 1 Churchgate Avenue
	8 Charlemont Parade	2 St Joseph's Square
	9 St Joseph's Villas	17 A2 1 Park Place
	10 Richmond Parade	2 Islandbridge Court
		3 Hospital Lane
		17 A3 1 Rosemount Court
		2 Turvey Avenue
		3 Rowerstown Lane
		4 Kearn's Place
		5 Carrickfoyle Terrace
		6 Prospect Terrace
		7 Millbrook Terrace
		8 Ashmount Court
		17 B1 1 Sullivan Street
		2 Black Street
		17 B3 1 Willie Bermingham Pl
		2 St John's Cottages
		3 Irwan Court
		4 Irwan Street
		5 Shannon Terrace
		6 St Maignenn's Tce
		7 Owens Avenue
		8 Almeida Avenue
		9 Ceannt Fort
		10 Auburn Terrace
		11 Knocknarow Tce
		12 St John's Terrace
		13 Traynor Place
		14 Lorne Terrace
		15 Mill Brook
		16 Camac Terrace
		18 C1 1 Thor Place
		2 Montpelier Gardens
		3 Temple Villas
		4 Tomar Court
		18 C2 1 De Burgh Road
		2 Park Avenue West
		18 C3 1 McDowell Avenue
		2 Kilmainham Village
		3 Prior Hall
		4 Mary Aikenhead Ho
		18 D1 1 Houghton Terrace
		2 Sitric Place
		3 St Mary's Tce
		(Arbour Hill)
		18 D2 1 Wood Lane
		2 Hendrick Place
		3 Viking Harbour
		4 John's Street North
		5 Hendrick Lane
		6 Ellis Court
		18 D3 1 Rainsford Avenue
		2 Marshalsea Lane
		3 Marrowbone La Bldgs
		4 Marrowbone La Close
		19 A1 1 Fitzwilliam Pl Nth
		2 Stanhope Street
		3 Catherine Lane Nth
		4 Father Matthew Sq

5	Smithfield Terrace	
6	Marmion Court	
7	Friary Grove	
8	Kevin Barry Flats	
19 A2 1	Burgess Lane	
2	Coke Lane	
3	Lincoln Lane	
4	Morgan Place	
5	St Audoen's House	
6	Oliver Bond House	
7	Wormwood Gate	
8	Usher's Lane	
9	Mullinahack	
19 A3 1	Brabazon Square	
2	Gray Square	
3	Meath Square	
4	Reginald Square	
5	St John's Avenue	
6	St Margaret's Ave	
7	Brabazon Street	
8	Coombe Court	
9	Hanover Street	
10	Park Terrace	
11	Spitalfields	
12	Liberty Square	
13	Meath Market	
14	Ash Grove	
15	Crostick Alley	
16	Flag Alley	
17	Engine Alley	
18	Pimlico Cottages	
19	Poole Street	
20	Widow's Houses	
19 B1 1	Lurgan Street	
2	Yarnhall Street	
3	Constitution Hill (Flats)	
4	Linenhall Street	
5	Henrietta House	
19 B2 1	Essex Gate	
2	Exchange St Lwr	
3	Meetinghouse Lane	
4	Ormond Place	
5	Hamilton Court	
6	St Michan's House	
7	St Michan's Lane	
8	Cork Hill	
19 B3 1	St Francis Square	
2	Davis Place	
3	Schoolhouse La W	
4	St Audoen's Terrace	
5	Borris Court	
6	John Field Road	
7	Longford St Great	
8	St Michael's Hill	
9	Christchurch Sq	

10	St Michael's Close	
11	Iveagh Bldgs	
	(Bride St)	
12	Lord Edward Court	
13	Whitefriar Gardens	
14	Hanover Court	
15	Power's Square	
16	Clarence Mangan Sq	
17	Bride Close	
20 C1 1	Findlater Place	
2	Strongs Court	
20 C2 1	Litton Lane	
2	Abbey Cottages	
3	Adair Lane	
4	Bedford Row	
5	Asdill's Row	
6	Merchants Arch	
7	Fownes Street Lwr	
8	Cecilia Street	
9	Crampton Court	
10	Parliament Row	
11	Champion Quay	
12	Palace Street	
13	Meetinghouse Square	
14	Curved Street	
15	Temple Bar Square	
20 C3 1	Harry Street	
2	Chatham Lane	
3	Balfe Street	
4	Coppinger Row	
5	Chatham Row	
6	Clarendon Market	
7	Longford Street Little	
8	Longford Lane	
9	Whitefriar Pl	
10	Glendinning Lane	
11	St Andrews Lane	
12	Johnson Place	
13	Clarendon Row	
14	Chatham Row	
15	Tangier Lane	
16	Glovers Court	
20 D1 1	Frenchman's Lane	
2	Moland Place	
3	Spencer Row	
4	Marlborough Place	
5	Northumberland Sq	
6	Deverell Place	
7	Talbot Lane	
8	Gandon Hall	
9	Custom Hall	
10	Marlborough Court	
20 D2 1	Corn Exchange Pl	
2	Rath Row	
3	Bracken's Lane	

4	Brunswick Villas	
5	Cards Lane	
6	Leinster Market	
20 D3 1	Nassau Place	
2	Molesworth Place	
3	Kildare Place	
21 A2 1	Magennis Square	
2	Peterson's Court	
3	Lombard Court	
4	Trinity Square	
5	Countess Markievicz House	
6	Westland Square	
21 A3 1	Wilson's Terrace	
2	Merrion Close	
3	Cumberland Court	
4	College Lane	
21 B1 1	St Laurence Pl East	
2	Blythe Avenue	
3	Ferrymans Crossing	
4	Bellman's Walk	
21 B3 1	Island Villa	
2	Greenore Terrace	
3	Rostrevor Terrace	
4	Pearse Grove	
5	Clanwilliam Square	
6	Clanwilliam Terrace	
7	Hogan Place	
8	Albert Place East	
9	Conway Court	
22 C1 1	Carbury Terrace	
2	Irvine Cottages	
3	Church Place	
4	Church Avenue	
5	Church Row	
22 C3 1	Ormeau Street	
2	Waterside Flats	
3	The Anchorage	
22 D2 1	Fisherman's Wharf	
2	Alexandra Quay	
3	Cambridge Square	
22 D3 1	Cambridge Court	
2	Canon Mooney Gdns	
3	Parkview Place	
4	Herbert Place	
5	Philomena Terrace	
6	Veronica Terrace	
7	Magdalen Terrace	
8	Strasburg Terrace	
9	Tyrrel's Place	
10	Whelan House	
11	O'Rahilly House	
12	St Joseph's Tce	
13	Victoria Cottages	
14	St Mary's Terrace (Ringsend)	

15 Seapoint Terrace
16 Simpson's Lane
17 George Reynolds Flats
23 A3 1 Kyle-Clare Road
25 A1 1 Hybreasal
2 The Paddock
25 B1 1 Almeida Terrace
25 B3 1 Moracrete Cottages
26 C1 1 McCarthy Terrace
2 Colbert's Fort
3 Fatima Mansions
4 Rialto Place
5 Boardman's Lane
26 D1 1 St Margaret's Ave
2 Huxley Crescent
3 Spencer Terrace
4 Brandon Terrace
5 Our Lady's Close
26 D2 1 Priestfield Cottages
2 Priestfield Drive
3 Ellford Terrace
27 A1 1 St John's Street
2 Warrenmount Place
3 Geoffrey Keating Rd
4 Cow Parlour
5 O'Curry Avenue
6 Watkin's Buildings
7 Weaver's Close
8 Brabazon Place
9 Warrenmount
10 Weaver's Square
27 A2 1 St Greenville Parade
2 Sandford Park
3 Wolseley Street
4 Brainsboro Terrace
5 Griffith Square
6 Garden Terrace
7 Greenville
27 A3 1 Hatters Lane
2 Greenmount Square
3 Armstrong Street
4 Le Vere Terrace
5 Harold's Cross Cotts
27 B1 1 Old Mill Court
2 St Kevins Avenue
3 Iveagh Buildings
(Kevin St Upr)
4 Malpas Court
5 Cathedral View Walk
6 Church Lane South
7 Harry Court
8 Cross Kevin Street
9 New Street Gardens
10 Long Lane Close

27 B2 1 St Kevins Cottages
2 Rosedale Terrace
3 Kingsland Pk Ave
4 Florence Street
5 Walworth Street
6 Bloomfield Cottages
7 Janeville
27 B3 1 Greenfield Place
2 Fitzgerald Steet
3 Ashworth Place
4 Drummond Place
5 Grove Avenue
28 C1 1 Aungier Lane
2 Protestant Row
3 Montague Court
4 O'Neills Buildings
5 Camden Villas
6 Camden Buildings
28 C2 1 Camden Court
2 Camden Street Old
3 Camden Market
4 Richmond Villas
5 Gordon Place
6 St Ultan's Flats
7 Charlemont Gdns
8 French Mullen Flats
9 Richmond Place S
10 Harcourt Lane
11 Albert Terrace
12 Lennox Terrace
13 Portobello Place
14 Charlemont Place
15 Harcourt Green
28 C3 1 Observatory Lane
2 Lissenfield
3 Cheltenham Place
4 Bannaville
5 Garden View
6 Mountpleasant Pde
7 Walker's Court
8 Mountpleasant Tce
Upper
28 D1 1 Fitzwilliam Court
2 Ely Place Upper
3 Mackie's Place
28 D2 1 Convent Place
2 Pembroke Place
3 Sussex Terrace
28 D3 1 Dexter Terrace
2 Mountpleasant Pl
3 Mander's Terrace
4 Mountpleasant Villas
5 Crosbie House
6 Willbrook House

7 Cullen's Wood
8 Osbourne Tce
29 A1 1 Convent Close
2 Baggotrath Place
3 Fitzwilliam Pl Little
29 A2 1 Wilton Court
29 A3 1 Warwick Terrace
2 Berysted
3 Mitchell House
29 B1 1 Cranmer Lane
2 Love Lane East
3 Grattan Ct East
4 Mount St Cres
5 St Mary' s Lane
6 Clanwilliam Court
7 Grattan Hall
8 Bridge Court
29 B2 1 Eastmoreland Pl
29 B3 1 Morehampton Square
2 Morehampton Mews
3 Ardoyne House
4 Hampton Court
30 C1 1 Lansdowne Tce
2 Emerald Cotts
3 Lansdowne Villas
4 Lansdowne Cres
5 Berkeley Mews
6 Beggars Bush Court
7 Haddington Way East
8 The Square
9 Canon Mews East
30 C2 1 Shelbourne Lane
2 Lansdowne Gdns
3 Carlton Villas
4 Herbert Cotts
5 Dodder View Cotts
6 Estate Cottages
7 The Sweepstakes
30 C3 1 Ballsbridge Tce
2 Pembroke Pl
(Ballsbridge)
3 Granite Place
4 Zardoz Court
30 D1 1 Havelock Terrace
2 Lansdowne Hall
3 Barrack Lane
30 D2 1 Railway Cottages
2 Martin White Chalets
3 Homelee
4 Claremont Court
30 D3 1 Prince of Wales Tce
2 Lynton Court
3 Spafield Terrace
4 Adair